Laurent
Clerc
The Story of His Early Years

Laurent
Clerc

The Story of His Early Years

Cathryn Carroll
with Harlan Lane

Kendall Green Publications
Gallaudet University Press
Washington, D.C.

Kendall Green Publications
An imprint of Gallaudet University Press
800 Florida Avenue NE
Washington, DC 20002

08 07 06 05 04   9 8 7 6 5

Cover illustration by Lucinda Levine, Washington, D.C.

Frontispiece attributed to John Brewster, Jr., *Portrait of Laurent Clerc,
1817-1820.* Reprinted with permission of American School for the Deaf,
Wadsworth Atheneum, West Hartford, CT.
Page 173: *Portrait of Laurent Clerc, 1822.* Charles Wilson Peale, artist.
Reprinted with permission of American School for the Deaf, Wadsworth Atheneum,
West Hartford, CT.

Library of Congress Cataloging-in-Publication Data

   Laurent Clerc: the story of his early years / Cathryn Carroll
with Harlan Lane.
        p. cm.
   Summary: A fictionalized autobiography in which the voice of
Laurent Clerc describes his boyhood in France as a deaf student
and his development of his own progressive methods to teach the
deaf.
   ISBN 0-930323-23-8
   1. Clerc, Laurent, 1785–1869–Juvenile fiction. [Clerc,
Laurent, 1785-1869–Fiction. 2. Teachers of the deaf–Fiction.
3. Deaf–Fiction. 4. Physically handicapped–Fiction.] I. Lane,
Harlan L. II. Title.
PZ7.C23483Lau   1991
[Fic]-dc20
                                                    91-7548
                                                      CIP
                                                       AC

Contents

Acknowledgments

I wish to extend special thanks to Kitty Fischer and Clayton Valli, who read most of this manuscript; Ben Schowe, Jr. and Sarah Val for their support and ideas; Donna Walls and Mike Olson for their generosity and patience in helping me through the Gallaudet University archives; Winfield McChord and Frank Asklar, for taking me through the museum and archives at the American School for the Deaf; Cindy Bailes and Victor Galloway, for first-hand reports about the acquisition of spoken language and reading skill in deaf children; Annick and Pierre Janty and Alexis Karacostas; Harlan Lane, who taught me so much; and Angela, Rachael, and my mom and dad.

1

"He'll Never Be Right"

"Laurent, hurry up!"

I couldn't make out the words exactly on my mother's lips. But I knew what she was saying. She was already fastening her cloak. Outside, the carriage stood ready. My father was giving instructions to the driver.

I tugged at my shoes and pretended to rush, but I was in no hurry. I was six years old, old enough to hate trips to the doctor. I hated the big hands on my face, the tugs at my chin and earlobes, and the rough edges of instruments pushed into my ears. I also hated the way the doctor shook his head when he was done—like he had something in his mouth that tasted bad.

Most of all, I hated how my mother cried.

Something was wrong with me. I didn't know exactly what, except that I lacked talent with my mouth. Other people's mouths sent messages. It seemed so easy. They aimed their mouths at each other, wiggled their lips, sometimes got a lump in their throats, and a message transpired. They even tossed messages to one another's back. They still caught them. My brother François used his mouth a lot.

I always watched. But I couldn't understand messages; I couldn't send messages either. When I tried, François laughed and my mother looked embarrassed.

Sometimes, I knew, people aimed messages at me. I would see their heads turn and lips move. I would see laughter. I never knew what I did that was so funny.

I had known something was going to happen. My father usually ignored me, but several nights ago, he called me to his side. He looked at me strangely, brought his face close to mine, and moved his lips until his face turned red.

I knew he was trying to send me a message. I missed it, of course, but I understood that it was serious. I nodded.

Then mother, who usually went to church three times a week, started going every day. Most of the time, I went with her. It was more fun than staying at home. I liked the church. I liked its darkness and I liked its smell. I even liked the small man in a robe who presided there.

It was boring, though, after the first few minutes, and I preferred to play outside. No one seemed to mind. Sometimes, I explored the caves in the surrounding hills. Sometimes, I just sat and watched the river. Mother would come to look for me when she was ready to leave.

Yesterday, I had become restless and gone back to the church to look for her. I found her kneeling, the robed man at her side.

When he saw me, he helped my mother up, and they both came to me. The man took my face in his hands, closed his eyes, and moved his lips. Finally, he made a cross on my forehead with his fingers.

On the way home, I tried to ask my mother about it. I really wanted to know why that man was holding my face and making a cross on my forehead. I think my mother tried to understand me. She stared at me for several moments. Then she looked away.

I don't know why I tried to send her messages. She never understood me. The gestures my brother and sisters and I used to communicate were still a mystery to her. She only understood messages from the mouth.

When we got home, I asked François. François always seemed to know everything. When he returned from school, I grabbed his arm and demanded his attention. He let me turn him to face me and watched me with the patience that made me love him.

I gestured at our mother and the chair where our father usually sat. Something was wrong with both of them, I indicated. The house was in an uproar.

"What's going on?" My whole body asked the question.

Unlike my mother, François understood my gestures immediately.

"Doctor," he signed.

He used the gesture we had invented ourselves, pretending to draw a mustache on his lip and then outlining a huge stomach with his hands—a perfect description of my first doctor.

His face didn't say "awful," like it usually did when he—or I—said "doctor." But I felt sick to see the word. Why was he smiling? He knew how I hated doctors.

I turned away to express my annoyance. He restrained me, trying to keep my eyes on him. For some reason, he was excited about this trip.

"Faraway," he signed, extending two fingers to arms length, another sign we had invented together.

"Famous," he said this word, I think, as he tried to act out greatness and respect.

He stood before me looking hopeful and happy. "Cheer up," his grin seemed to say. "This doctor will be different. The strangeness will go away. Mother will not cry afterward. You will send messages and understand them, too."

I didn't believe it. For a moment, though, I tried to smile at him.

I finished putting on my shoes and raced to the carriage, trying to make up for my tardiness with a show of speed. My father ignored me. He was gentle to my mother, though, helping her up to the seat and kissing her cheek. Then we were off. As we headed down the familiar street, I thought again about François. I hoped he was right to be so cheerful.

The carriage rolled out of the town and I nestled against my mother. Her eyes were closed and her lips moving. For a long time I looked out the window.

Finally, I saw the outline of a city. It was Lyon, I would learn later, a great city in southern France. At the time, I didn't know the name of that city, or my country, or even my hometown, La Balme. I only knew that François might be right. Perhaps in this grand place, a doctor could be found who could do what other doctors could not. I felt a ray of hope.

The carriage moved slowly through the city. From my window, all around me seemed to be confusion, a tangle of carts and carriages. There were many busy people, most of them moving their mouths and gesturing fiercely at each other.

I felt more hopeful when we pulled up to a large door in front of an imposing house. A woman greeted us, not warmly but efficiently. Standing next to my mother, I waited and watched, encouraged and nervous.

Then I saw the doctor.

He was a big man, old with very white hair and skin. As he moved his mouth, his blue eyes gazed at the ceiling or roamed around the room. He looked at my mother for only a few moments. He didn't look at me at all. Other doctors waited until they had examined me to get that "bad taste" in their mouths that contorted their facial features; he seemed to have it from the beginning.

At first, the exam was the same as all the others. The large doctor peered and pulled and explored with his huge fingers, while my mother sat and watched.

My hopes dwindled.

The doctor's assistant appeared from a side door. He was younger and smaller than the doctor, with a face like a mouse. The doctor and his assistant moved their mouths at each other. Then they moved their mouths at my mother. My mother stared at them a moment. Finally, she nodded.

The assistant went into another room and returned with a tube filled with fluid that looked like dirty water. It must have smelled bad, for the men turned their faces from it, and my mother buried her nose in her handkerchief. The assistant gave the tube to the doctor, who shook it and stared at me. His lips moved a bit.

I knew this must be the famous healing medicine. Without looking at me, the assistant took my head in his hands. He turned my head sideways. I stood very still.

The tube rested against my ear a moment. Then, the doctor squeezed the end of the tube and fluid gushed deep inside my ear, filling the side of my head with pain. Some of the fluid splashed down my neck and wet my collar.

I tried to pull away. The assistant propped his elbow against my shoulder and held me tightly. Then, as if he had finished shearing one side of a sheep and was ready to start the other, he thrust my head to the other side. Helpless, my whole body followed. A dose of liquid burst into my other ear.

I screamed and tried to kick and claw my way free. Other hands—I think that they were my mother's—joined in restraining my body.

I don't know if they released me or if I pulled away. Suddenly, I was free. I ran across the room, screaming and crying, and holding my throbbing head. The room looked funny and my stomach felt upset. It was a long time before I allowed even my mother near me. She held me tightly against her as we made our way out to the waiting carriage.

I cried until I caught sight of La Balme, my own village. My mother gently stroked my cheek. I raised my eyes to her and she smiled at me. She looked pleased, I thought. She extended her hand and I took it.

I began to feel hopeful again. Perhaps I had not failed the test this time. Perhaps I would be cured.

At first, the pain was all I could think about. My head hurt so much I couldn't walk straight. I felt like a bent, little, old man, scared that someone was going to try to force me to run or jump.

Gradually, the pain faded. After two days, my eyes stopped burning and my walk returned to normal. I was not ready to play, though, and I ignored my sister's teasing. She wanted me to chase her. I stayed in a chair, resting my head against its high back.

I was confused. The famous doctor had attacked my mouth problem by way of my ears. There must be an important clue in that, I guessed. Ears and mouth must be related.

Lifting my head, I beckoned to my sister. I brought her head down to my level and placed my lips near her ears. I had seen François do this. It was one of the many ways he seemed to send messages. My sister bent over expectantly and waited. Then I moved my lips— and everything inside my throat and chest—with all my strength.

I was more successful than I intended to be. My sister snapped her head away from me, jumped back, and pushed me away. She looked angry; her mouth and hands worked furiously. She approached me, once, and swatted my shoulder. But, she seemed afraid to stay near me and, still working her hands and mouth, ran from the room.

Astonished and a little pleased, I sat back in my chair. So the doctors were right. The mouth and ears were linked. What a discovery! This knowledge was worth my sister's anger and the renewed pain in my head.

François, standing by the window, had seen everything. He laughed. Then he came over and rubbed my shoulder. I laughed with him, elated. We were so happy.

I had sent my first message. Perhaps the new medicine was working.

The next day, the feeling returned that something was about to happen. As usual, everyone but me seemed to know what it was.

We had just come back from church and my mother refused to let me change my clothes. She didn't change her clothes either, and the carriage remained outside our door. It appeared that we were going out again. I looked for François but couldn't find him.

I did find my sister. I waved my arms to get her attention. Then, looking puzzled, I pointed to my clothes and through the window to the carriage.

"Why am I dressed up?" I was asking. "Where am I going?"

"Faraway doctor," she signed back, matter of factly.

At first, I thought she was confused.

"Finished," I signed back.

I had already been to the faraway doctor. Thank God it was over.

Again, I pointed to the carriage. But my sister had known what I was asking.

"Faraway. Doctor. You," she said and left the room.

I understood. I was going back to that same doctor in Lyon that very afternoon. More powerful medicine in powerful doses would be forced into my ears.

In the next two weeks, I returned to the doctor three more times. Always, he did the same thing to my ears—pulling, peering, prying, and pouring in the liquid. Always, I promised myself I would be brave. Always, when the liquid seared into my head, I screamed and cried.

I hated the doctor for doing this to me. I hated my mother for bringing me to him. And I hated myself for being what I was.

After the last visit, I waited for my mother in the carriage while she talked to the doctor. She cried the whole way home. I tried to feel relief, but a gloom had settled over our house. My mother, so happy before, looked sad again.

The triumph of startling my sister was not repeated. I knew that my ears, as well as my mouth, were broken. I couldn't send messages except for simple ones with my eyes. The great medicine from the great doctor in the great city had failed.

A part of me still hoped. Someday, I told myself, I would surely be like other people. Most of me knew, though, that I would always be the way I was. There was no cure for me.

Much later, I learned what the doctor had told my mother. I don't know the details, of course. All I know is what François told me when we were both grown men: The learned doctor had looked at my mother after his treatments that had been as expensive as they were painful and told her, "He'll never be right."

2

Leaving Home

They left me alone now. At least there were no more doctors.

I took care of my father's horse or shooed the turkeys out to the field. I knew more about the nearby caves than anyone in the village. My sister, who feared the darkness of the caves and their winding passages, would only go there with me.

Years passed. I was twelve when I learned that I was being sent away. I did not know where and I did not know why. I only knew that the maid had packed my clothes, all of my clothes.

I tried to ask François about it, grabbing his arm as he ran through the house. He paused a minute, looking confused. Then inspiration struck.

"School," he responded. He reached over to where his own school books lay and tossed me one. I caught it.

"Why tease me?" I gestured, hurt and angry, and even more puzzled. He knew as well as I that I could never go to school. It was the message problem. Even my sisters got to go to school. But I stayed home, forever ignorant, with my mother.

François grinned at my puzzled face. "School. You. Yes," he cried and gestured.

He clapped me on the shoulder and ran on. His friends were waiting for him outside.

The next day, my mother returned from church and François returned from playing with his friends at the same time. The maid brought my suitcase to the front door. My sisters stood on one side. François stood on the other. Then my father came home. He had not really looked at me since that day so many years ago when I returned from the doctor in Lyon. He still didn't quite look at me, but he kissed my cheeks.

My mother, dressed in her best clothes, took me to the carriage station. To my surprise, my uncle showed up and greeted us. A little younger than my father, he was red-faced and cheerful. He traveled a lot, I knew. This time, it appeared that I was going with him.

My mother started to cry. I felt her body shaking as she hugged me good-bye. I was too scared to cry. I was a little curious, too. My uncle and I entered a carriage with other travelers. I was the only child, and my uncle made sure I sat by the window. I watched my mother grow smaller as the carriage bumped down the street.

My uncle slapped my leg, grinned, and nodded at me. Whatever we were doing clearly had his approval.

We rode all day. When the sun sank low in the sky, and it was almost dark, the carriage pulled up to a huge house. Many carriages with teams of horses were lined up outside. Inside, men sat at long tables, drinking, eating, and talking.

The men seemed to have a lot to say. So did my uncle. He laughed and moved his mouth and I wondered if he had met these strangers before. With all the excitement, I planned to stay up all night. I fell asleep almost immediately, though. I slept until my uncle woke me at sunrise.

We boarded another coach and traveled on. The land changed. We kept traveling. Each evening, the carriage stopped at a huge house. Each night, I vowed to stay awake, and, instead, I fell quickly and completely asleep. Each morning, as the sun rose, my uncle shook me awake and our journey continued.

If François were with us, I might have been able to find out where we were going and how long we would travel. But, with my uncle, I remained ignorant. I was content, though. My uncle smiled a lot, knew to touch me to get my attention, and checked to see that I wore enough clothes to stay warm. I was comfortable in silence with him next to me.

We traveled for five days. I knew we were approaching a city when my uncle began to call my attention to the increasingly close together signposts and the road began to swell with people. I had learned the names of Lyon and La Balme through the signposts. Now I learned the name of a new city—Paris.

Nothing had prepared me for the immensity of Paris. Compared with Paris, Lyon was a carriage stop. We never really entered the city; it just stretched out and swallowed us. The streets were clogged with people and carriages. The streets were dark, too, thrust into shadow by grand buildings, rising higher than I imagined possible.

Sometimes, my uncle pointed at them and moved his mouth at me. I couldn't catch his messages, but I caught his excitement. I nodded, smiling. I was excited, too.

We inched slowly forward. It was like crawling through the intestines of a giant.

We changed to a smaller carriage, almost like the one we had at home. My uncle and I were the only passengers. My uncle gave some money to the driver and moved his mouth and pointed. The driver nodded, and we were off.

After a while, I noticed my uncle and the driver seemed confused about where we were going. Neither seemed to agree with the other, and both their mouths had curled up tightly. Around us, everything had changed.

The buildings were still high, the streets, narrow and filled with people. But the city was not splendid here. People were dressed more simply, their clothes were dirty, and sometimes torn. Paint peeled from the buildings, and the shutters hung precariously, often by a single hinge.

We stopped several times. My uncle and the carriage driver exchanged messages with people walking along the streets. It seemed as though we drove in one direction and then in another.

Finally, we stopped at a battered gate and I saw, by my uncle's face, that this would be our resting place for the evening. The sun hung stubbornly in the sky, but I was tired and glad to stop early in spite of the oddness of the lodging.

A wall, dirty and chipped, surrounded it and there were no carriages outside. Through the gate, I saw a huge building, beautifully made, but almost without paint and without glass in most of the windows.

"Need carpenter!" I tried to joke with my uncle using gestures.

I was not surprised that he ignored me. He got out of the carriage, spoke with the man at the gate, and showed him some papers. The gate swung open. The carriage rolled into a small courtyard.

Another man scurried out and greeted us. My uncle shook his hand and handed him my valise. I went to get my uncle's valise, but he shook his head. I tried to insist. He firmly motioned me away.

Fear rose in me. My uncle's face had lost its smile. He looked thoughtful and even a little sad. As we followed the man inside the dilapidated building, his eyes examined the stones at his feet. He didn't look at me.

My fear grew. Surely he would not leave me here. I was too big to grab his hand, but I clung tightly to the edge of his sleeve.

The man led us down a dim hallway into a small, dark room, where a fire blazed. There were chairs, but neither my uncle nor I sat down. My uncle paced back and forth, his hands behind his back, his eyes on the floor. I stood in the corner near the fire and watched him.

It seemed like we waited for a long time. Finally, a door opened and a man entered the room. He was tall and thin, and had curly hair that hung to his shoulders. He shook my uncle's hand and nodded. Then he shook my hand. No one had ever shaken my hand before.

I was amazed. I had feared a doctor. But this man was no doctor. For one thing, he wore strange clothing, expensive, but tattered and old-fashioned. Around his waist he wore watches—not one, but many.

It was not his clothes or all the watches that interested me. It was something else. His gentleness, maybe, and his eyes, which were clear and very blue. They looked right at me, too.

This man didn't use his mouth. He and my uncle exchanged messages with a slate and chalk, like the ones that my brother and sisters took to school. They took turns, each scribbling purposefully, then passing the slate to the other.

Finally, the man pulled a piece of paper from the desk and my uncle reached over and signed it. They stood up and shook hands.

I moved closer to my uncle. My uncle turned and hugged me. Then, like my mother had done, he burst into tears.

Scared, I cried, too. I hung onto him and begged him in every way I knew to take me with him. How could my mother have sent me here? How could he leave me so far from home with this stranger?

Still crying, my uncle took his hat and rushed from the room. I tried to run after him. But the tall man prevented me and closed the door. I tried to force my way past him, but he caught me.

I couldn't fight him. He was as strong as he was gentle. He kept my hands away from the door and my fists away from him. Through it all, he looked at me kindly and a little sadly.

After a while, he pulled out one of his watches and held it out to me. His manner told me that the watch was a special prize and I should feel privileged to look at it. I wasn't curious. The watch wasn't as big as my father's, nor as ornate as my uncle's. I couldn't understand his fascination.

In my puzzlement, though, I stopped crying. He smiled at me and led me out of the office. My eyes looked down the hallway toward the courtyard where I thought my uncle might still be waiting in his carriage. But the door to the courtyard was closed. I followed the tall man as he walked in the other direction.

The man led me to a small room and I peered inside. Boys a little older than I were sitting at desks. A priest stood next to one of them. He was bent over, pointing back and forth between the boy's slate and his opened book.

I remembered the book François had tossed to me. My brother was right. This strange place was a school.

The man started to lead me up a staircase but stopped and seemed to change his mind. Instead, he beckoned me through another doorway.

In the open courtyard, a group of boys were playing on the stone pavement. They had a hard little ball, which they were rolling toward a group of upright sticks.

I had often seen boys play this game at home. Sometimes, François even made the boys let me join them. These boys were skilled players, I realized, watching the ball roll again and again into the sticks, knocking many of them over. Two men, one of them a priest, watched from a corner.

Suddenly, an argument broke out. I knew it was an argument because the game stopped. The boys' faces looked angry. Two boys kept grabbing for the ball at the same time. An older boy took the ball and held it aloft, while hands flew back and forth grabbing for it.

Finally, without moving from where he stood, the man next to the priest lifted his hands and motioned for the boys attention. The boys stopped quarreling and turned toward him. His hands waved in the air for a few minutes. The boys exchanged more hand movements among themselves. Faces relaxed. The older boy tossed the ball back onto the courtyard stones, and the game resumed.

Somehow, I knew that they were talking with gestures. Their gestures were much faster and smaller than
the gestures my brother and sisters and I used at home.
Our family gestures were easier to understand, too.
François almost acted out his messages. So did I.

A stranger could sometimes guess at the meaning of
our family signs, but no stranger could understand
these swift movements. But the man in the corner had
understood—and wiggled his fingers back at the students. These movements were as much a mystery to me
as my family's mouth movements.

Suddenly, the older boy noticed the tall man and me
and pointed to where we were standing. The game
slowed and then stopped. All of the boys ran over to
us. The tall man raised his hands, made gestures, got
their attention, and sent them a message. I watched the
merriment and laughter.

I felt the boys were a bit impolite. A number of them
pointed several times right at me. The tall man didn't
stop them, either. He seemed to think pointing was
normal.

He put one arm on my shoulder and held up his free
hand. His fingers did a light dance in the air. The finger
dance was repeated by the other boys, each of them
raising his hand and performing it. Sometimes, a boy
stopped in the middle and looked up toward the man.
He would nod and show the boy how to go on.

When everyone had gone through the dance, another
topic arose. I was still at its center it seemed, for they
again pointed at me. The older boy touched his forefinger to his ear and then to his mouth, all the while
pointing at me. The man nodded.

I did not have the word then, but I knew what he
was saying: Yes, they were broken, my ears and my

mouth. No one seemed to mind. They were nodding at me excitedly.

The older boy stepped close to me and ran two of his fingers along my cheek. His eyes returned to the man, and the same two fingers stroked his own cheek.

I knew what that meant, too. Feeling embarrassed, I put my own fingers to the scar on my face. I had gotten the scar as a baby. François told me that I had fallen into the cooking fire in my home, tumbling into the unprotected flames. My mother ran over and scooped me up. She had always blamed the fall—and probably herself—for my broken ears and mouth.

I traced the lines of the scar and watched the group continue its conversation. They seemed to like that scar. Several hands traced its imaginary outline on their own faces. The only visible sign of the long-ago fall, it marked the easiest and quickest way to focus on me.

Then I was officially introduced to the other boys. At a signal from the tall man, each boy pointed to himself, danced his fingers in the air, then made a simple, easy-to-remember gesture. The oldest boy cupped his hand on his chest; the boy with freckles held outstretched fingers against his shoulder; still another boy pointed his index finger at his cheek. I nodded at each boy, who then stepped forward and shook my hand.

The last boy wiggled his fingers and flashed a hand movement at me. I nodded and stroked my fingers along the scar on my face. They were delighted. I had made the motion mostly out of nervousness. I realized that the scar had become more than a part of my body. Now it signaled my name.

I wondered about the tall, still man next to me. I turned to him, pointed at his chest and looked, puzzled, into his eyes. Who was he?

He grinned. Then he raised his hand, which he held very still while his fingers danced in slow motion, one movement following the next. "J-E-A-N M-A-S-S-I-E-U," he must have spelled, for I would learn to spell in this place. I would learn that the finger dances were simply the spelling of the alphabet by the hands.

The tall man flicked his hand against the back of his neck as if he were pushing back his long hair. He repeated the motion and I copied it. Looking very pleased, he nodded and clapped me on the back, the same way François did when he was happy with me.

He gestured toward the boys. I watched a volley of other hand movements. The oldest boy took my suitcase. The tall man waved good-bye. I mounted the stairs with an escort of boys.

I was in a daze. I had been in the school less than an hour. Already, I had learned so much. I knew gestures for each of the boys; I knew the gesture for the tall man; I knew the gesture for myself, too. I had learned that hands—as well as ears and mouth—were the vehicles of messages, and I had seen the quickest hand-message system I could imagine.

I had learned something else, too. With my index finger, I touched my ear and my mouth. The two broken parts of my body that had caused me so much pain. The gesture meant "deaf." I was only days away from writing the word. I was **deaf**. So were all these people around me—the tall man and all those boys. They were smart and friendly and played ball as well as any of the boys in my village.

I also knew that this place was not just a place to eat and sleep for the night. This was the place for which my valise had been packed.

3

A New Life

The older boy, I learned quickly, was Pierrot Janty. Pierrot was our monitor, a senior student who helped the new students learn the rules and made sure that all of the students obeyed them.

It was Pierrot who had carried my valise up the stone staircase and into the large room where fifty boys slept. Fifty beds lined one wall; fifty washstands another. A blue-and-white uniform lay on the bed, waiting for me. It was not new, but it was clean. Pierrot indicated to me that it would be altered to fit me.

The next morning, I failed to get up on time. I suppose someone shook me. I was used to rising with the sun, not before it. I remember opening my eyes to a murky scene of boys and bedlam. But it scarcely felt real, and I drifted back to sleep.

It was not the way to further a friendship with Pierrot. He came over to my bed and shook me himself. When I did not respond, he shoved me off the bed and onto the floor. The fall didn't hurt; I hardly felt it. I even tried to keep on sleeping, but the stone floor was too cold.

The other boys were dressed and at the washstands. No one noticed me as I hurried to catch up. From across the room, Pierrot waved at me and grinned.

Pierrot whacked the boys who disobeyed and sent those who were late for church or class to bed without supper. With unfailing energy, he criticized everything—Parisians, the school, its rules, the other students, and, sometimes, even the French government and the priests.

Pierrot's personal opinions, though, never kept him from doing his job. I saw him swing into action in the first week I was at the school, just after dinner. His victim was Claude Wallon, a new student like myself, who was there on scholarship. Claude was thin and shy, with enormous brown eyes.

I sat next to Claude, so I saw him try to sneak a piece of bread from the dining room. He was headed for the courtyard when a priest stopped him.

"What are you doing?" The priest pulled up Claude's clenched fist. We could see the bread sticking out of either end of his hand.

Pierrot rose from the table and marched over to the priest and Claude. Without breaking his stride, he smacked Claude's outstretched hand. The morsel of bread flew across the room.

Claude, small next to Pierrot and the priest, hung his head and put both fists in his eyes. Pierrot argued with the priest a bit. At least, I think they were arguing, I couldn't understand the hand motions well enough to know what they said. I assumed it was about Claude's punishment.

Claude, who knew as little about the hand language as I did, continued to cry. Finally, Pierrot tapped his shoulder and told him he could go. Claude fled into the courtyard. I wanted to go to him, but I was too scared to get up.

I knew why Claude had tried to steal food; he was hungry. We all were. We'd had little to eat all week.

Only once, at lunch, had we been served meat—tiny bits of gray mixed in a muddle of vegetables. That evening, we'd had soup for dinner, brown-colored water with small bits of floating material.

"Goop from the cook's greasy spoon," complained Pierrot.

"Pieces of bugs," suggested Claude.

I didn't know. I was so hungry, I would have eaten anything. I took the single piece of bread we were served and slid it around the sides of the soup bowl. I drank my entire glass of wine and swallowed my cheese in a single bite. When the food was gone, I felt as though my dinner had not even begun.

I had never known hunger before. At the school, I would be hungry often. The first week was only the beginning. There was never enough food.

There was never enough of anything. In class, we shared slates and chalk. My book was so old and worn that some of the ink had disappeared, and, in some places, whole words were unreadable.

There wasn't enough coal, either. In winter, we were always cold. We shivered through classes. We shivered through meals. We shivered in our sleep.

Sometimes my parents sent me a little money. I was always grateful. It meant I could buy bread or fruit on the streets of Paris. But for Claude, and the other students on scholarship, there was only hardship.

Pierrot blamed the Directory, the group of people who were, for a brief period, the government of France.

"It was better under the king," he told Claude and me.

Pierrot used small tight signs and looked nervously about as he made them. Claude and I looked around, too. We thought we were alone, but we could never be sure. Pierrot could be killed for talking to us like this. We could be killed, too, for letting him.

Our country had suffered a revolution, a strange and terrible war that French people waged against their own royal rulers. I was eight years old when we learned that people—Parisians—had arrested and finally killed our king and queen. François told me about it. When the news reached La Balme, my mother spent the whole day in church. Even my father stayed home and didn't work. I thought that it was surely the end of France and perhaps the end of the world.

It wasn't. In La Balme, our lives continued as before. In Paris, people continued to die. When Pierrot was my age, he watched carts filled with doomed people pass the school on the way to their deaths on the guillotine. Every day, those carts rolled by, he told us. Thousands had died.

"Blood filled the street gutters like rain water," commented Pierrot.

I knew nothing about the new government, except that Pierrot hated it. The Directory was just the newest group of murderers, he told us.

"They rule in the name of brotherhood," he said in his whispered signs, "but they give us nothing."

Worse, the government hated priests—all priests— including Abbé Sicard, our school's famous director, who had almost been killed during the revolution and was now in hiding. If he came back to the school, or appeared publicly anywhere in France, he would be arrested and probably killed.

"Why doesn't the government like Abbé Sicard?" asked Claude.

"Because he loves God," answered Pierrot, firmly. "And he loved the king."

Looking at the walls that surrounded the school, I wondered what would happen if the killing started again. In my village, I could run into the woods or hide in a cave. Here, I was trapped. If the government wanted to find me and kill me, I would be dead for sure.

I was thinking of my mother. I didn't think of her often. Only when things went wrong, or late at night. Lying in the darkness, I sometimes ached with thoughts of her.

I missed François, too. When I thought about them, I missed my brother and my sisters. I even missed my father. In fact, I missed every person and every house in La Balme.

I missed my freedom, too. In La Balme, I could walk where I liked. I could wander through fields, along the river, into the caves. Here my life was boxed in behind the school walls. Every moment was planned. Every step was watched. At home, I was often alone. Here, we lived as a group. As a group, we awoke, dressed, ate, and went to class, mass, and into the surrounding city. As a group, we studied and went to bed.

At home, I was part of a respected family. Here I was just another first-year boy in a blue-and-white uniform. I suppose the priests felt love for us. It was like God's love, I guess, extended equally to everyone.

I missed girls and women, too. Here there were only boys and men. The girls lived and went to class in a separate building. It was just across the street, but it might as well have been in another country. We only saw the girls on Sundays when they joined us at church.

If my mother knew what it's like here, she'd be sorry, I thought, lying in my bed.

However, even in my homesickness, I liked school. Mostly, I think, because of the signs. Signs, I knew now, were the gestures we used when we wanted to talk. We made signs with our hands and fingers, and with our faces and bodies.

I learned sign language quickly. Everyone said so. After a few days, I could talk easily with the other students. After a few weeks, I could watch the boys across the courtyard and understand their conversation.

After so many years of struggling to make my thoughts known, suddenly I could express myself as effortlessly as I could breathe. I could understand others with equal ease. It was a great luxury.

I got good grades, too. Actually, from my first day, I was at the top of my class. Jean Massieu, the tall man who had admitted me, became my teacher.

I adored Jean Massieu. Perhaps I loved him so much because of our daily encounters in his classroom. Claude, myself, and six other new students sat in three rows, while Massieu directed his thoughtful gaze among us.

We learned the alphabet first.

"A," began Massieu. He held up his fist, his thumb resting against his bent fingers. Then he scratched the same letter on the slate board.

"B," he continued. This time he pointed four fingers skyward and crossed his thumb over his open palm. On the slate board appeared a vertical line with two humps.

At our desks, we imitated both ways of making letters, continuing through the alphabet until we slashed the air with our pointed index fingers and our slates with the chalk, making "Z." I was thrilled.

I had often watched my father writing. For me, it was like communion, a kind of holy rite that I never dreamed of understanding, let alone doing myself.

Massieu showed us that, with twenty-six simple letters even children can learn to make, a person could write any word in the French language. In two days, I could make every letter on my fingers and get from A to Z in two minutes by Massieu's watch. In two weeks, I could write each letter.

The first words I learned to write were my own name.

"Everything has a name," explained Massieu. "People, things, ideas, parts . . . parts of parts. Each name has its own spelling and usually its own sign."

We stared at him intently.

"As deaf students, you need to study especially hard to learn all these names," he continued. "Hearing people know the names of everything."

"Only because they use the names when they talk," Pierrot commented that day at dinner. "It's not a big accomplishment."

"How did they memorize all the names?" Claude was awed.

"They memorized nothing," Pierrot was indignant. "Hearing people ignore the letters and say the word as a whole sound, like we sign. The hearing know the words, the deaf know the signs. It's the same thing."

"So the messages I see on people's lips are just hearing people strewing together all the names?" I asked.

"Exactly! Who knows what they strew together?" exclaimed Pierrot.

Across the room, seated with the table of deaf staff, sat Massieu. Seeing his eyes on us, I asked for confirmation.

"Is he right?" I signed in the space between the heads that separated us.

"Mostly," Massieu nodded. "That's why hearing people can read and write so easily. It's their own speech they see on the printed page. Each letter has a sound. They just make the sound of each letter as they see it. Reading is just seeing their talking in print."

For us deaf students, it was much harder. We had to learn French, a language we couldn't hear, at the same time we learned to read.

It was important, we knew, so we worked very hard. Massieu crammed words into our heads, twenty-five to thirty words every day. At first, they were simple words: pen, slate, desk, teacher. Massieu would show us the object, fingerspell its name, write that name, and show us the sign.

I was lucky; I memorized easily. Some students missed recess and trips to town, choosing instead to study their ever-growing word lists. Claude often studied his words at dinner. Once, a bit of soup splashed onto his paper and soiled it, hiding some of the letters in the words he was trying to learn. From across the room, Massieu frowned. From across the table, Pierrot reached over and rapped Claude's knuckles.

I never saw Pierrot study. I worried that he wouldn't pass his senior year. Pierrot, though, wasn't concerned. He spent his time laughing, joking, telling stories, and punishing us. He complained so much about the school and the priests that, for a long time, I couldn't understand why he was a monitor.

Every day after lunch, Pierrot and Claude played ball in the courtyard with the other students. I didn't join them. I had been picked to be in Abbé Magaron's speech class, held only during afternoon recess. I didn't mind missing the games. Only the smartest boys were asked to be in the speech class and I felt proud to be among them.

The first day I went to class, Claude just smiled, but Pierrot shook his head as we parted.

"The only thing more stupid than written French is spoken French," Pierrot grumbled. "And the only thing more stupid than a deaf boy trying to speak is a deaf boy trying to speak for Abbé Magaron."

"Abbé Garlic-Breath," Claude smiled softly as he signed the teacher's famous nickname.

I stared at them hard for a moment, not knowing what to say. I would try anything in order to be able to speak aloud. I didn't have the heart to defend my decision. But I wasn't going to change it, either.

As I turned to go, I saw Pierrot's comment clearly from the corner of my eye. "They'll never understand him," he told Claude. "Not even when he asks for bread at the bakery across the street."

Blushing, I climbed the stairs rapidly and almost bumped into Massieu, who was returning to his apartment from his classroom. He clapped my back and grinned. I had gotten the highest score in the class on my vocabulary test, he told me.

I smiled and blushed even more. I don't know why I felt so shy around him. I tried to think of something to answer, but no words would come. He didn't seem to need any words from me.

"Smart boy," he complimented, then continued down the stairs.

Heartened, I marched on to Abbé Magaron's speech class. I hated it, of course. All of us did.

Abbé Magaron was old and bad tempered. The boys said that he smelled of stale wine and garlic. Worse, he tried to compensate for the invisible grindings and vibrations that make up speech by opening his foul mouth as wide as possible. It seemed the circumference of a small carriage wheel. Looking inside was painful. I winced and watched.

"It reminds me of the caves near La Balme," I joked to Pierrot. "Big wide entrance, narrow inside, and a squiggle hanging off the roof."

Pierrot had heard of the abbé's mouth. It shared equal fame with his breath.

"Why don't you get a scalpel from the infirmary and trim his tonsils?" he laughed. "That should keep it closed for a while."

Of course, we boys were as distasteful to Abbé Magaron as he was to us. He never smiled. His face flushed often and was especially ugly when he was angry. In the doctor's office, I could be still while they picked, probed, and pronounced me a problem. In speech class, I seemed to contribute to my failure. When we boys made mistakes, Abbé Magaron's face would get even redder and his eyebrows would converge above his eyes. He hit us, too. He said that it helped our pronunciation. Nevertheless, those first weeks I was hopeful and happy.

Pierrot and Massieu recalled that there was a deaf Frenchman who had once learned to speak perfectly. Massieu told us that the man stopped talking as he grew older, but that he had impressed everyone with his perfect pronunciation when he was young.

So, I tackled Abbé Magaron's class with determination and I tackled Jean Massieu's class with zest. I would endure Abbé Magaron and enjoy Massieu. I would put up with Abbé Magaron's bad temper and revel in Massieu's kindness.

As one day faded into the next, I felt thrilled with the information that poured into my soul. I would make my mother, and even my father, proud of me. Let the other boys play ball. I would learn to read and write and I would learn to talk.

4

Home Again

Summer came, and I returned home.

My visit started out wonderfully. The countryside welcomed my uncle and myself as we retraced our earlier journey, traveling from inn to inn, toward La Balme. In a light breeze, trees waved their branches, seemingly in greeting. My mother and sisters met us at the carriage station. They hugged me and cried.

After Paris, La Balme was small and quiet, but it was beautiful, too. Our house glistened in the sun. I couldn't believe how happy I was to be home again.

When I walked in the door, François jumped out from behind the door and threw his arms around my neck. We hugged each other ferociously. Everyone welcomed me and seemed to admire me, too. Only my father looked at me skeptically.

And the food! People tell me that food has a smell like voice has a sound. I can't smell and I never miss it. But, if there were one meal that I wish I could have smelled, it was that first meal of summer vacation.

It was a feast. We had ham, deer, fish, potatoes, small carrots, and a salad of summer vegetables. Best of all, we had butter and all the bread anyone could want.

As soon as my father had said grace, I filled my plate and fell to eating. I didn't look up until I finished, only to see my family talking serenely to each other, most of their food still before them. I felt embarrassed. They had barely started to eat. My sister giggled, but my father rebuked her with a glance. My mother said something to her, too. François looked over and translated for me.

"You're too thin," he gestured.

My bad manners were excused. When I had a second helping of everything, that was excused, too. I ate more slowly this time, making the food last as long as I could.

The next day, we went to the chapel by the caves. I was surprised how small it was. Yet it felt as holy as the huge cathedrals I had seen in Paris. I understood more about church now. As the priest talked and prayed, I thanked God for sending me to a place where I could learn, keeping me safe, and letting me come home.

I glanced at my father and, for the first time, felt that I pleased him, at least a little. Perhaps it was the good report I had received from school.

François told me what the report said. "You learn quickly. You study hard. You're a good student!" he interpreted proudly.

My glowing pride and happiness faded slowly. First, routine replaced it. In some ways, it was like I had never left. I did chores for my mother and father. François, who had been my constant companion during my first days back, became busy again with his friends. It was no easier to include me now than before. I returned to being alone. Alone, I visited the caves, and alone, I walked by the river.

It was not quite the same as before, though. I felt a new restlessness. I felt uncomfortable with my aloneness now. Sometimes the discomfort was vague, like morning fog. Other times, it was heavy, like an overfull sack I couldn't get off my back. Sometimes, it nudged me; other times, it was overwhelming. It was always there.

I think it was because I no longer liked being alone. Also, for the first time, I resented being "the deaf one."

At school, my deafness was no more a problem than having two legs. At school, my deafness meant nothing. Here, it meant everything.

Perhaps if a person lives his whole life in the cold, he stops noticing it. But if he happens by a fire, he remembers. Now I remembered the warmth of easy communication. I remembered my friends.

I was less patient than before, too. Our family signs were rigid and slow compared to the signs I had learned at school. My brother and sisters didn't want to learn these new signs I loved so much. I showed some to François and he agreed that they were faster and better. But, he still refused to learn them. To him, it wasn't worth the trouble.

Only my mother seemed to find me a joy. And she, more than anyone, had reason to doubt me.

We were returning in the carriage from Lyon, when my mother first tried to talk with me. She had brought a slate for this very purpose. Now she wrote some words on the slate and passed it to me.

"How do you like school?" My mother had written.

I stared. I looked from the words to my mother's face. She looked so happy and expectant. It was such a short message. How could I tell her that I was not sure what it meant?

I could almost understand it. The last three words "you like school" were easy; I understood that. "Did" is the past tense of "do"; I knew that. "Like" and "you" were switched around because the sentence was a question; Massieu had taught me that.

But "how" was one of those words that mystified me. There was one sign for "how many" and another sign for "how." The signs, though, rarely provided clues to the meaning in written French.

Trying to show a confidence I did not feel, I took the chalk and neatly answered the question.

"Yes," I wrote.

Her face fell. I knew it was the wrong answer. My mother looked at me with the same puzzled expression as when the doctors had examined me. After a few minutes, she took the chalk again and wrote more words: "How was your trip?"

Again, I stared. Did every question in French begin with "how?" (None of them did in Massieu's classroom.) I wasn't sure what "trip" meant either. We had learned the word "journey" in class, but the more conversational word "trip" had never been in a vocabulary lesson.

I felt sweat on my forehead. Finally, in desperation, I wrote, "Clerc happy." She seemed content then.

Later, though, we had another misunderstanding.

A few weeks after I returned home, an elderly neighbor woman came to the door very upset. My mother and sisters talked to her for a minute and then prepared to leave with her.

Before she went out the door, one of my sisters turned to me and explained that the woman's husband had fallen and she wanted some help getting him up.

She also gestured that I was to begin preparing dinner. She and my mother would cook it, of course, but I was to help get the food ready.

She started to tell me more, but my mother approached with the slate she often carried. She had written these instructions: "Before I cook the carrots, please peel them."

I was a little angry that they wanted me to help with what was clearly a girl's job. They never asked François, I thought. But, I was the only one home, and I really had nothing else to do. I looked at the slate and nodded.

They were only gone for a short time, but that was enough. I didn't really try to read the message on the slate. As always, I was unclear about what the words meant. I had never worked in the kitchen, and I had no clues to help me understand the words before me. I knew the word "cook"; I knew the word "before"; I knew the word "carrots"; I guessed what "peel" meant from my sister's quick gestures.

I performed the tasks as my mother wrote them. I boiled the carrots in water. Then I tried to peel them.

"Laurent, what are you doing?" my sister cried on returning. I couldn't hear her, but I saw my name on her lips and her horrified expression.

I was scraping the cooked carrots, trying unsuccessfully to separate the peel from the flesh.

Seeing my embarrassment, my sister burst out laughing. My mother, though, looked shocked and disappointed. They sent me from the kitchen and threw away the carrots.

At dinner, no one talked about it. No one seemed to care that their food arrived a little later than usual and that they weren't having carrots.

I felt terrible. That night, as we sat by the hearth, my old feeling of guilt returned. I wasn't only alone; I was deficient. In my mother's glances there was love and caring, but no belief that I would ever understand.

5

Pronouns and Printing

I was glad to get back to school.

Massieu was my teacher again. Pierrot continued as my monitor, Claude as my classmate. Claude and I had been promoted from the fourth level to the third level.

I was glad Claude was still in my class. I had been worried that he wouldn't be promoted, or, even worse, wouldn't return to school at all. He was excellent at math and drawing and expressive in his use of sign language. Yet he failed almost every test in French.

While I attacked print passionately, Claude avoided it. Even when he studied, he seemed to forget vocabulary as quickly as he learned it. Despite our constant conjugating of verbs, Claude seemed to throw dice to decide what endings to put on verbs.

I blamed Pierrot. The older boy had a strong influence on all of us, and Pierrot hated French.

"French is not worth the trouble it takes to learn," he often said. "It has no logic. It's stupid."

Pierrot, if he had been treated like the other students, would have graduated the year I arrived. Instead, he made his first communion and returned to the senior class. Communion was delayed for all of us. We had to learn to understand how to communicate before we could learn about religion. The main purpose of our education was to bring us knowledge of God and the holy sacraments.

Pierrot was still our monitor. He was as outspoken as ever. His uncle, I had learned, was a rich merchant who gave large sums of money to the school. Even so, I wondered why the priests let him stay.

Pierrot thought signs were better than French. One day at lunch, he told Claude that if deaf people knew signs, they did not need French. The priests ignored him. Only Massieu, watching from the table where the deaf staff sat, reacted.

"If Abbé Sicard were here, you'd not talk that way," he scolded.

I waited until it was time to go to bed to ask Pierrot about a sticky aspect of French that continued to bother me. I wanted to know about pronouns. We had studied them in class that day and I had found myself totally confused.

Massieu had begun by listing them on the board: I, you, he/she, we, you, they. Looking at the words, my confidence grew. For a boy used to stuffing twenty-five to thirty words into his head, this was easy.

"I," said Massieu and pointed to himself.

"You," he said and pointed to me.

"He," he said and pointed to another boy, keeping his eyes on me.

Then it was my turn. We had had pronouns last year and this class was a review. I thought that I understood them.

"I," I mimicked, pointing exactly as Massieu had, to Massieu himself.

"You," I continued. Again mimicking Massieu, I pointed to myself.

"He . . ."

Of course, Massieu stopped me. I was completely wrong. Yet, when I saw Massieu shake his head, I thought at first that he had misunderstood me. Then followed one of the most convoluted lessons that I have ever been privileged to not understand.

All of us boys stood in a circle. We pointed at Massieu, at ourselves, at each other. Sometimes, Massieu was "he"; sometimes Claude was "he"; sometimes I was "you." By the end of the lesson, I had figured out that only I could be "I," but only when I said so.

"I don't understand this," I complained, showing Pierrot my senseless notes by the light of his candle.

"It's not your fault, Clerc," he told me bluntly. "It's French. French is not logical."

I'd heard that before . . . at least one hundred times.

"I know." I smiled at him. "Signs are logical."

"Yes," he affirmed immediately, "by using signs it's easy."

He rehearsed the words in sign, pointing matter-of-factly to himself, to me, and the boy in the next bed. Then he repeated his motions, only fingerspelling immediately after each point.

A point at me was "Y-O-U," he told me.

I couldn't help myself. I stopped him, puzzled. In the circle, sometimes I had been "Y-O-U," but usually I had been "H-E."

"Boys are always 'he,' or 'him,' " I rehearsed.

It was Pierrot's turn to look puzzled.

"I'm not talking to any boy," he continued. "I'm talking to *you*. Y-O-U."

I shook my head and he lost his patience.

"I'm not talking about *him*," he signed, gesturing with exasperation at the boy in the next bed. "I'm not talking about *him*," he pointed to Claude across the room. "I'm talking to *you*. *You*. Y-O-U."

"Clerc, forget it," signed a sleepy boy.

"Yeah, Clerc, it's time to sleep," Claude urged, moving near a wall-based candle so I could see his signs in the darkness.

"Stop!" Pierrot signed sharply "You—Y-O-U (he pointed to Claude) and you—Y-O-U (and he pointed to the boy in the next bed). Clerc's here for school. And—(he jerked his thumb toward me, then he fingerspelled quickly) "H-E can ask me any question he wants."

Suddenly, he looked at me and grinned.

"Understand? Do Y-O-U understand about pronouns Laurent Clerc?"

It took me a minute.

"Yes," I finally answered. At least I understood better.

"So much . . ." I searched for the sign I wanted, "arbitrariness."

I looked at Pierrot. He threw up his hands.

"Signs do make more sense," I added sheepishly, as he put out the candle.

Most of my out-of-class learning was in the print shop. I liked machines and I liked words. I found myself under the watchful eyes of Jean Massieu, setting up and running the enormous printing presses. Taking turns, we students assembled the letters and inked them, fitted the paper, and lifted and lowered the press. We printed ten, twenty, and sometimes fifty copies of textbooks and study sheets. We printed all our school's materials and two journals for teachers. Occasionally, we printed announcements for nearby merchants and even, sometimes, for government officials. It was our job to make sure the machines stayed in top condition, and the papers we printed were clear and readable.

"Why do hearing people always put deaf people down?" I asked Massieu one day as we cleaned up.

"Because they're idiots," Pierrot replied firmly.

"Because they think we're stupid," added Claude.

"Because *they're* stupid," Pierrot was unwavering.

Massieu laughed softly. "Do you know that, in English, mute and stupid are the same word?" he asked, with the absent-mindedness of a philosophy teacher.

"What?" I couldn't believe it.

One of the books my parents had sent me was on the English language. One never knew what those strange people across the Channel—and their cousins across an ocean—might come up with. But, even for them, it seemed absurd.

Massieu was scratching his head, trying to remember the English spelling. "D-U-M-," Massieu paused. " 'B' or 'D,' I'm not sure which."

Pierrot had turned away in boredom and disgust, but I found myself practicing the spelling and rehearsing the word with my hand still at my side.

"It's an ancient belief that deaf people can't learn," Massieu continued, turning to me. "Only in modern times has it been proved wrong."

"By Abbé de l'Epée when he founded our school," Pierrot completed Massieu's thought.

Massieu looked at Pierrot and shook his head.

"No," he said slowly.

"The first man to teach deaf students was deaf himself."

Claude and I stared doubtfully. Pierrot made a face as if he thought Massieu were joking.

"I'm serious." Massieu looked amused at our disbelief.

"Who?" Claude asked.

"Étienne de Fay." Massieu fingerspelled the name precisely and looked at us for a reaction.

"Who was he?" I asked, becoming exasperated.

"A man shrouded in mystery," responded Massieu, a twinkle in his eye.

We waited.

"I really can't tell you a lot." Massieu was serious now. "De Fay was born a long time ago. No one knows exactly when, perhaps around 1675.

"His family was rich and noble. I don't know how his family felt about having a deaf son. They must have wanted him to get an education, though, because they sent him to school in a monastery in Amiens—"

"Wait! Where?" I reached out to stop Massieu's hands. The word had literally flown off his fingers.

"Amiens. A-M-I-E-N-S. It's in northern France." Massieu paused a moment and looked at us. "He learned from the monks and became a monk himself.

"He was brilliant," Massieu continued. "De Fay understood geometry, mechanics, design, and history. He became an architect and designed new buildings for the monastery. He sculpted, too, and carved faces of the saints on statues inside the monastery. He also wrote and illustrated books.

"And at the same time, he taught deaf students, perhaps six or seven at a time."

We were fascinated.

"When did he become deaf?" asked Claude.

"He was born that way," answered Massieu.

"Born deaf?" Claude was pleased.

"Yes, like you." Massieu smiled at Claude.

"Did Abbé de l'Epée learn from him?" I asked.

Massieu shook his head. "By the time Abbé de l'Epée decided to start our school in Paris, de Fay had long been dead. People forgot quickly about the small school in the monastery," Massieu concluded.

After pausing a moment, Massieu continued, "Abbé de l'Epée's teachers were two deaf sisters."

We laughed. The thought of the saintly abbé learning to sign from two deaf women was too much for us.

"It's true," Massieu protested, understanding our laughter and challenging it gently.

"Abbé de l'Epée was a man who became a priest and then refused the priesthood. He learned signs from the deaf to become their teacher."

Pierrot rolled his eyes. What was our teacher trying to say?

Finally, Massieu told us the story of the founder of our school, the man most responsible for deaf education in France.

"Michel de l'Epée was born to a wealthy family. His father was an architect at Versailles, and de l'Epée spent his early days at the beautiful castle of the French king near Paris. By the time he was seventeen years old, he was ready to become a priest.

"No doubt the priesthood would have welcomed such an earnest young man from a prominent family. But, in the end, de l'Epée refused to take his vows.

"At that time, the church was requiring all priests to condemn a certain group of Christians, the Jansenists. As a student of the priesthood, de l'Epée had to sign a paper saying that all the Jansenists were condemned to hell. He refused."

"What's a Jansenist?" Claude asked. I had never heard the word, either.

"Jansenists either believe that the body of Christ is part of the body of God, or that the body of God does not contain the body of Christ." Massieu shrugged, as he always did when faced with religious dogma. "I can't remember. It's not important."

"So Abbé de l'Epée was not really a priest?" I was amazed.

"Maybe not technically," answered Massieu, "but he was a priest in spirit. He helped everyone. Right from the beginning, he used his own money to help people. Born rich, he died almost penniless."

Massieu continued the story. "One day, Abbé de l'Epée entered a dingy apartment in one of the poorest parts of Paris. Inside, he found twin sisters sewing quietly at a large table. The abbé introduced himself, but the two girls ignored him. Not understanding, he sat down and waited for their mother to return home.

"He thought they were just shy. Really, they were two deaf girls who had to put up with this strange hearing man who had appeared, without invitation, in their living room."

Claude and I looked at each other and laughed.

"When the girls' mother returned," Massieu continued, "she told Abbé de l'Epée how worried she was about her two deaf daughters. Of course, her biggest concern, like Abbé de l'Epée's, was to bring them knowledge of God to save their souls."

"Priests . . ." Pierrot cut off our teacher, signing the word like it was an oath.

"Abbé de l'Epée was a true man of God," Massieu corrected him, although Pierrot was scarcely looking at him. "He wanted to do good on this earth.

"He told the mother to send the girls to his home for

religious instruction. When the girls showed up at his home, Abbé de l'Epée decided to learn their signs.

"He reasoned that, if the girls could talk to each other, they could talk to him," Massieu continued. "All he needed to do was learn their language. . . ."

"He really learned sign language?" Pierrot was finally interested.

Massieu hesitated.

"Well, not really," he admitted, "but he learned the signs of sign language, and some of the nouns and verbs."

"And invented classroom signs!" Pierrot was aghast.

So Abbé de l'Epée was the culprit.

"He invented a way to put signs into French word order and make signs match the French language, so you and I and Claude and Clerc here could learn . . ." Massieu stopped at the look of torment on Pierrot's face.

"Classroom signs!" My friend sighed. He shook his head.

"Signed French," Massieu corrected gently.

"French is important, Pierrot," I ventured.

"From Abbé Magaron's star pupil," he answered sarcastically.

I blushed, not comfortable with the direction of the conversation.

"No one is smarter than the times he lives in," our teacher pointed out.

6

The Shepherd Genius

The only time I saw Jean Massieu show strong emotion was when he talked about our absent director, Abbé Sicard. Massieu thought that Abbé Sicard was a saint. Often, he told us of all the wonderful things this holy man had done for deaf people. Massieu credited Abbé Sicard with saving his soul.

"I was nothing before I met him!" he declared.

Pierrot, looking up from printing a pamphlet we'd started the day before, rolled his eyes. Outside, the weather remained stormy, though this afternoon pale ribbons of sunlight seemed ready to break through the clouds hanging low in the skies.

"What do you mean, you were nothing?" I asked.

Massieu looked at us a moment before he replied. "A human being is nothing without learning," he stated.

Pierrot rolled his eyes again. "Abbé Sicard was nothing without you!" he protested with sudden vehemence. "First, you made him director, then you saved his life. Soon, you'll have him returned from exile."

Massieu looked at his passionate advocate and laughed. "You exaggerate Pierrot," he responded gently.

But Pierrot couldn't help himself. "Abbé Sicard would be nothing without you," he signed again.

Massieu's smile vanished. I could see that he was getting angry.

Pierrot saw it, too. He turned back to the press, his face flushed and his hands trembling slightly.

I wanted to keep them talking, but I didn't know how. Claude did, though.

"Massieu, you always tell us about Abbé Sicard," he nudged Massieu shyly. "Tell us about you."

Massieu's anger vanished. He smiled suddenly and ruffled Claude's hair.

"I've told my story," he shrugged.

It was true. It was part of the performance that he and Abbé Sicard gave for our hearing audiences. Once, he told it to a special meeting of the most learned men of Paris, called The Society of the Observers of Man, in a fancy salon in a fancy club.

"Please." On either side of him, Claude and I begged to hear. We had not yet seen the performances.

Reluctantly, he began. "I was born twenty-nine years ago, in Semens, a small village . . ."

Massieu had five brothers and sisters, all of them deaf like himself. His parents were hearing, like mine. Like me, he and his brothers and sisters invented a sign system that they used in their home.

Also like me, Massieu wanted more than anything else in the world to go to school. His father, like mine, refused to let him. As deaf children, he and his brothers and sisters could only watch as the other village children trooped past on their way to school. Perhaps his brothers and sisters didn't mind missing school, but Massieu was devastated.

"I begged my father to teach me," he told us. "I wanted to read. When he refused, I begged more. I cried, and I screamed, and I pleaded. I got a book from the shelf in our home and turned it upside down over my head.

"I did it to show my ignorance. I wanted the words to spill out and wash over me. My father was firm. School was not for a deaf boy."

Once, Massieu sneaked out of the house and went to the town's schoolmaster.

"I begged to join his class," Massieu remembered.

The schoolmaster was as firm as Massieu's father and less kind.

"He was angry and disgusted with me," Massieu signed. "I was wasting his time, a worthless boy with a stupid hope."

As an adult, Massieu was not bitter about either his father or the schoolmaster.

"They believed what most people believed," he explained. "There was no way to teach deaf children."

Unlike me, Massieu came from a very poor family. He had worked from early childhood, watching his family's flock of sheep, until a stranger appeared.

"God, himself, must have brought that man to my fields," he said. "God must have seen how much I wanted to learn. He must have pitied me."

Massieu remembered the stranger in exquisite detail—the lines in his face, his gloves, the scratches on his boots, and his narrow brown eyes. But he hadn't the foggiest idea of his name.

"I never knew it," he told us calmly.

Somehow the stranger and the deaf shepherd boy held a conversation. The stranger knew about a school for the deaf in Bordeaux, a city about the size of Lyon that was near Massieu's home. The Bordeaux school was started by priests from the Paris school. Its director was Abbé Sicard.

I wondered if Massieu's father was as relieved as mine when he left for school. He was older than I had been. He was fourteen years old.

"I learned quickly," Massieu told us, "like Clerc." And he smiled at me.

I blushed and lowered my eyes to hide my pleasure and embarrassment. Pierrot and Claude pushed at me, teasing, shaking their heads and smiling.

Claude noticed that the print on the papers had become a shade lighter. He got a new bottle of ink. Massieu stopped him from adding it to the press.

"Too much money," he said. "Let's print a few more light ones."

"What happened at the school?" I urged Massieu to continue, not wanting the story interrupted.

"Saint Sernin, a priest in the school, was my teacher. He had worked with Abbé Sicard and used Abbé Sicard's teaching methods."

The distinction between Abbé Sicard and Saint Sernin was never important to Massieu. It was as if Abbé Sicard were the brain and Saint Sernin the hands of a single person. What was important was that he learned. He learned to read, write, and do arithmetic. More important, he learned about God.

"Before, I thought the sky was God," he told us now. "I would pray to the sky."

Massieu walked over to the window. I followed him and looked out. The storm had broken. In the courtyard, the trees bowed under the swift wind and the first, hard drops of rain.

"I didn't know then about God, or Jesus, or the Blessed Virgin," Massieu said. "The sky seemed very strong. I prayed every night. Sometimes I prayed to the stars, especially one star.

"I prayed often to that star. Once a relative was sick. I didn't know him well, but my mother did, and I hated to see her so sad. She refused to eat, couldn't sleep, and cried at meals. So every night I prayed to the star to make him well.

"When my relative died, I blamed the star and threw stones at it."

He paused and looked at us. Indeed, we were surprised at his imagination and boldness.

"Then I was scared," he smiled and shook his head, remembering. "I was afraid the star would punish me, perhaps even kill me."

Pierrot and Claude and I shook our heads, too, amazed.

"Abbé Sicard showed me the error of my beliefs. I came to know God," he said. "Now I love and worship only Him."

Outside the rain splashed against the window. I looked out to see sunlight fighting with the storm and white rings around the low clouds. I thought about the pictures in the chapel of the saints in their robes. Those people carried light around their heads, too, like those undecided clouds.

I could understand praying to the sky. I could understand praying to the earth, too. I looked across the room where Claude had again stopped the presses and was cleaning a heavy accumulation of ink from the wooden letters. I could even understand praying to a printing press.

Massieu saw my stare and smiled. "Abbé Sicard saved me," he signed simply when my eyes returned to him. "It's only through learning about God and the sacraments that we can be saved. Abbé Sicard saved my soul."

"And you made him famous!" Pierrot couldn't help himself.

For Massieu was not just one of the first educated deaf people in France. Massieu was a genius. When people met him, or when he was questioned before audiences in public presentations, his responses filled people with awe. His language was that of a poet; his understanding, that of a seer.

So, Pierrot insisted that it was Massieu who had helped Abbé Sicard and not the other way around. Pierrot said that Massieu even won Abbé Sicard his job as director of the Paris school.

"When the Abbé de l'Epée died," Pierrot stated, "the school needed a new director. Abbé de l'Epée had named an assistant to succeed him and the government would probably have accepted it," Pierrot maintained, "except that Abbé Sicard, in faraway Bordeaux, wanted the job."

Abbé Sicard wrote a letter and proposed that the government have a contest and that the winner of the contest be the new director of the school. Abbé Sicard suggested three candidates. All of them were men, all were priests, and all were teachers of the deaf. Each would bring one of his students to the contest. The priest who showed he was the best teacher would get the job.

"The man who was the best teacher was, of course, the man with the best student," Pierrot concluded. "The best student in the whole world, deaf or hearing, had to be Massieu. And Abbé Sicard knew it."

"So Abbé Sicard won the contest and got the job?" Claude asked.

"There never was any contest," Massieu the gentle teacher hauled his enthusiastic student back to the facts. "The other two priests refused to compete. Abbé Sicard got the job by unanimous decision, an act of God . . ."

"Default," snapped Pierrot.

A touch of anger again passed over Massieu's face. I tried to divert him.

"Was Abbé Sicard a good teacher?" I asked.

"The best," answered Massieu's hands.

"The worst," replied Pierrot's hands at the same time.

As they were both Abbé Sicard's students, Claude and I looked at each other and laughed.

"Abbé Sicard didn't really teach you," Pierrot insisted, looking at Massieu. "Saint Sernin was your teacher."

We turned to Massieu expectantly. A correction never came. Finally, Massieu lifted his hands and signed again.

"Saint Sernin was my teacher," he said finally. "But Saint Sernin worked with Abbé Sicard, and it was Abbé Sicard's method we used. By his leadership, Abbé Sicard is a great teacher."

Pierrot threw up his hands in exasperated triumph. Afraid to look at Massieu, he made tiny signs in the direction of Claude and myself.

"Abbé Sicard can't sign," he confided.

Massieu, who had read the signs from the corner of his eyes, was furious.

"The abbé signs French," he insisted sharply. Then he signed something—I'm not sure what—in those horrible classroom signs.

Pierrot just shrugged.

7

Speech Class

A storm was brewing as I hurried to speech class. I glanced at the courtyard where the boys were trying to finish a game of ball before the first drops of rain fell. Pierrot was right, I thought. This class was becoming tiresome.

Abbé Magaron, my speech teacher, promised that talking would help us understand French. Massieu seemed to agree.

"Hearing people learn to read so easily," Massieu said again and again, "because print is their speech in code."

I was making progress. But, I still had trouble with some sounds, especially the sounds "da" and "ta." These sounds looked the same on the lips and the tongue. Nevertheless, they sounded different.

"That's because with 'd,' you wiggle invisible muscles deep in the throat," I tried to explain to Pierrot. "With 't,' you hold those muscles steady and splatter your audience with spit. Or it's the other way around," I concluded lamely.

No matter how I tried I could never remember which sound did what. All I remembered was that they both looked the same, and with one of them, Abbé Magaron covered me with spit. I turned "dod" into "tot" and "dad" into "tat." I also made Abbé Magaron furious. He said that I forgot on purpose.

I arrived in the abbé's class to find him in a particularly fearsome mood. His face was red and his brows hugged each other above his eyes. Even before he got to the tricky sounds, the dreaded spit flew from his mouth.

"Have you practiced?" he demanded.

"Yes," I lied.

Actually, I never practiced. The only time I used my voice deliberately was in his class.

Obediently, I went through the exercises. I made it through most of the sounds. "B" and "p" play the same tricks as "d" and "t." Once, confusing them caused me to think that "baby" was "pappy." I had been heartily whacked. But I had negotiated this lesson perfectly so far. Yet, Abbé Magaron looked angry. In my fear of arousing him further, I became very nervous.

The dreaded "da" and "ta" sounds approached as I knew they would, and I began to sweat. I saw the abbé's lips move and he held up the letter "d."

I couldn't remember. Spit or vibrate. My mind was blank.

I looked down at my balled up, sweaty fist. I had written the letter that required spit on my palm before class. I didn't dare look. From math I knew that I had a fifty percent chance to get it right.

"Ta," I exploded, happy to see I had pushed some spit in the abbé's direction.

Whack! The blow was sudden and to the chin. My jaw snapped shut and my tongue, poised between my teeth, was nearly cut in half. I cried out and clasped my mouth with both hands. Blood filled my mouth and seeped between my lips and fingers. I had guessed wrong.

I looked to see the abbé's face contort further. His mouth opened and shut, his lips flapped, and spit flew in all directions.

I saw him pull back his hand for another launch at me. I jumped away and ran from class, holding my jaw with one hand, and wiping my tears and blood with the other. The abbé didn't come after me. In my memory, he is still shouting at me from his doorway, his face disgusted and triumphant, like a man who had just cleared his room of a crazed dog.

I ran down the steps. Outside, a light rain was falling, but the boys were playing ball still, enjoying the recess I always missed. I didn't want to join them. I wanted darkness. I wanted to hide. I wanted to be alone.

I headed for the classrooms. It was still recess, so they would be empty, I thought. But in the first one sat Massieu. He was bent over a small desk, reading a book that the seniors must have been studying.

I tried to slip past without him seeing me. He caught up with me and touched me. I turned to him and collapsed, still trying to hide my face, streaked with tears and blood.

Massieu rubbed my hair and let me cry. When I finally got enough nerve to look at him, his face—not his hands—asked what was wrong. I told him everything. Using his handkerchief, he wiped my cheeks and chin.

"I hate him!" I cried.

I was so humiliated I talked boldly, in a way that I knew could earn me another whack. But Massieu didn't look offended. He said nothing. Once he stroked my hair again.

I felt foolish. Massieu, I knew, never talked. I thought about his written exchange with my uncle on the day he admitted me, and how he conversed with hearing priests and teachers using a slate or a sheet of paper.

There was dignity in that, I thought. It was better than the grotesque sounds of labored speech.

I stole a glance at Massieu. He smiled.

"Who cares how you say a letter?" he asked almost absently. "What does it matter?"

I hugged him. My hands encircled his waist and, forgetting that I was bloody and wet from crying, my face pressed against his shirt. His hands rested lightly on my back.

Then he sent me to the washroom. By the time I showed up in the print shop, my mouth had stopped bleeding and my eyes had lost their redness.

"I learned a lot in speech class today," I announced almost heartily.

"Forget it, Clerc," said Pierrot, as he handed me a pamphlet we were printing, still wet from the press.

"Give us a break," agreed Claude.

Massieu looked amused as I told them the story, ending with its moral: "I learned that I'm never going to use my voice again."

I never did.

"Well, what do you think?" Claude was pointing to the broadside in my hand.

"Claude did the drawing," Massieu explained. "It's Bouilly. It's about his play."

The drawing was excellent. Claude was never paid for his work, but everyone was delighted with it.

With his artist's hands, Claude was an especially able printer. Often he suggested changing the arrangement of a piece we were printing so that each word could be set in larger type. He drew pictures for some of our customers and for the school's learning materials, too.

Our printing customers began asking for Claude. He almost never communicated with them directly. He never felt comfortable with people who used their voices to converse. Sometimes, Massieu would help him, using a slate, or a hearing teacher who knew signs would interpret.

I saw him work alone with the hearing customers, though, using gestures, pantomime, and sketches. People throughout Paris were beginning to seek out my shy friend. Soon he would be recognized as a truly talented artist.

"I'm no Goya," Claude protested modestly. Massieu had learned of Francisco Goya, the famous Spanish painter who had become deaf as an adult. The teacher had taken Claude to see one of Goya's religious paintings, hanging in the home of a friend.

Massieu turned back to the press and placed the last sheet of paper over the still-wet letters. Claude wiped off the excess ink.

"Claude will help us bring back Abbé Sicard from exile." Massieu was smiling.

"Because of your plan," Pierrot amended vehemently.

I waited until Massieu turned his back to ask Pierrot my question.

"What's his plan?" I asked gesturing toward Massieu. "How will he bring Abbé Sicard back from exile?"

Pierrot glanced at Massieu before he answered. Massieu remained bent over the press, facing away from us.

"Do you remember when Massieu asked Claude to sketch the man we saw in the square?"

I remembered. A few days earlier, the four of us had stopped in a café. A group of men had entered the café and Massieu had become very excited and walked right up to them.

We students didn't understand the conversation that transpired among Massieu and the men. We saw Massieu's slate pass back and forth. One of the men left the group and went into an artist's shop.

Massieu hurried over to us.

"Claude, your talents are required," he exclaimed. "We need you to make a sketch of the gentleman in the artist's shop. Can you do it?"

Before the astonished Claude could respond, the stranger returned from the artist's shop, paper and charcoal clutched in his hands.

Claude's surprise turned to delight. He accepted the new and fine materials. He beamed a "thank you" smile toward the patron and began to sketch him.

"Who is he?" I asked Massieu, as Claude sketched.

"Jean Nicolas Bouilly," Massieu answered swiftly. "The most famous playwright in Paris."

"Is he going to pay for Claude's work?" questioned Pierrot sharply.

Massieu's glance told him to settle down. Of course he wouldn't pay. Pierrot knew as well as I that payment was out of the question.

Quickly, as if his fingers were following lines already on the paper, Claude made a series of drawings of Bouilly's head. To our delight, the men bought us each a glass of wine while we waited. When Claude had finished, everyone gathered round and marveled. The men were clearly pleased.

"How much money will he be paid?" asked the imperturbable Pierrot again.

Massieu didn't answer. But later, when he and Pierrot were alone, he had explained. Now, Pierrot told us the story as Massieu stood by.

"Bouilly wrote a play about Abbé de l'Epée and our school," he started, excitedly. "The play shows that, for ridiculous reasons of politics, we have no director."

"Napoléon will never allow such a play!" I protested.

"He already did!" Pierrot was triumphant. "Napoléon himself was in the audience. His wife was there, too."

We gasped, astonished. But there was more. Pierrot continued excitedly.

"In the play, there's a scene where the actor who plays Abbé de l'Epée talks about how the school misses him when he is gone. Last week, when the actor said those words, some very brave men in the audience interrupted the play. They stood up and called for Abbé Sicard's return.

" 'We want Sicard! We want Sicard!' they yelled, right in the middle of the theater."

I must have looked doubtful for Pierrot's signs became faster and stronger. Massieu was watching him now, but he didn't seem to care.

"Napoléon Bonaparte, the great general who led the French army to victory, heard it," signed Pierrot. "He had to hear it."

Pierrot looked at our teacher.

"You planned it that way," he commented.

Pierrot explained that the night before the performance, Massieu and Abbé Sicard had gone together to the home of a famous Paris lawmaker. There they had met Joseph Bonaparte, brother to Napoléon and first consul of France.

"Abbé Sicard wasn't arrested?" I couldn't believe our director could be so brave.

"No, they didn't arrest him," Pierrot maintained. "He went under special protection. Massieu personally begged Joseph Bonaparte to permit Abbé Sicard to return to the school. He said that the loss of Abbé Sicard was a loss to all the deaf children in France."

I thought that was a little much.

Pierrot did, too, I think. But he didn't pause in his tale.

"Bonaparte must have believed him," he asserted, "because all three ended up in each others' arms, crying like children."

He paused to let this emotional scene sink in.

"It's just a matter of time. Soon Massieu will have Abbé Sicard free."

I was not surprised by this. I knew that since the abbé had been forced into hiding, Massieu had been working for his pardon and return. Claude and I looked at our teacher before we asked the last pressing question of Pierrot.

"Why do you always say Massieu saved Abbé Sicard's life?" I asked.

But it was too late. Massieu loved stories, but not when the audience and storyteller found him of more interest than the school's director.

"Clerc, we're done," said Massieu abruptly. "Clean the press."

Pierrot, catching the firmness, turned away. I ran for the cleaning fluid.

8

Our Flamboyant Abbé

One month later, Abbé Sicard was free.

The news spread rapidly through the school. Hands flew in the halls, courtyards, classrooms, and gardens with one glorious message: Bouilly's play was a success! France's famous priest and teacher, a hero in exile, Massieu's beloved friend and our blessed father, was coming back to us, his loving children and students. Abbé Sicard was coming home.

We gathered in the assembly room to welcome him. Students, teachers, staff, and all the finest people of Paris were assembled. Bouilly was there. So was the bishop and government officials, French nobility, and royalty from neighboring countries.

They crammed into the gallery above us, hundreds of them, the women, their hair piled high, and the men in frilly collars and morning coats. Outside, carriages filled the courtyard.

Even the girls from the deaf school were there. They sat on the other side of the room, their eyes downcast in shyness, but happy. All had gathered to greet the returning Abbé Sicard.

Massieu was so excited that he couldn't sit down. He walked back and forth, hands clasped behind his back, eyes aflame. He had skipped breakfast that morning. I don't think he'd eaten dinner the night before, either. He looked like a champion pony, anxious for a race to begin.

When Abbé Sicard entered, all heads turned toward him.

He didn't look like a teacher. He didn't look like a priest. Above all, he didn't look like a man recently returned from unhappy exile.

He was short and fat, and extremely well-dressed. His hair was long. He strutted as he walked, his puffed-out chest bedecked in a silken sash of shiny medals. His arms were outstretched in welcome. His nose was too long and his face seemed to slope over his tiny chin.

He looked proud, too, as he aimed his little chin toward the ceiling. He was like a poor noble, who wanted to look rich, I thought. He seemed very pleased with himself. He grinned as he walked, his eyes as shiny as the medals on his chest.

I turned back to Pierrot to make sure that this comic figure truly was Abbé Sicard. Pierrot's eyes were riveted on the stubby figure, making its way to the stage. I turned to Massieu, waiting on the stage. My heart sank. The sight of my ecstatic teacher was enough to banish any doubts. This man, indeed, was Abbé Sicard.

As soon as Abbé Sicard had mounted the stage, Massieu embraced him. The students waited a minute, then we were permitted to join them on stage. Some of the students cried; they were so happy.

As for me, I was busily trying not to show my disappointment. I tried to look grateful and enthusiastic. I crowded dutifully against the others. I kissed the abbé's hands, but not, as some students did, his knees and feet.

Even then, I was a little surprised by my reaction. Perhaps my expectations—birthed and bred by Massieu—caused my disappointment. I had expected to see a kind of Christ on earth. This man looked more like an unsuccessful shopkeeper.

For once, I thought, Pierrot may have been more right than Massieu. Perhaps he had even been one hundred percent right; perhaps the best thing about Abbé Sicard was his former student Jean Massieu.

Though they disagreed about the kind of man he was, I had learned a lot about Abbé Sicard from Pierrot and Massieu. He was born Roch-Ambroise Sicard, more than fifty years ago. He became a priest when he was twenty-eight years old and director of the school in Bordeaux when he was forty-three. Three years later, Abbé de l'Epée had died, and Abbé Sicard, riding on the coattails of Jean Massieu, became director of the Paris school.

Abbé Sicard knew that Massieu was an invaluable asset. Shortly after he became the school's director, he took Massieu and three other students to ask the French government for more money. At that time, the school had even less money than it did now, and some students had been sent home. It was Massieu who petitioned the government and asked that our school be made the national school for the deaf.

The National Assembly, France's first revolutionary government, which tried to bring life to the words, "liberty" and "equality," voted to accept Massieu's petition. Abbé de l'Epée learned the news on his deathbed. The National Assembly would pay for twenty-four students to attend the school and ten people to work there. It would now be known as France's National School for Deaf Youth, the first such school in the world.

Abbé Sicard had the school moved to a street called St. Jacques, on the Left Bank of Paris, the place where I, myself, was a student, and where it still stands today. Asked by Americans where I went to school, I would respond, the National School for Deaf Youth in Paris. But among ourselves, we French deaf always said simply that we went to "St. Jacques."

The good feeling between the government and the St. Jacques school didn't last. It was a period of revolution and emotions were strong. Sicard made no secret of his loyalty to his king and his God. The French government—the National Assembly, the Legislative Assembly that took its place, then the Directory, and finally Napoléon—hated both.

Abbé Sicard had edited a newspaper for priests. The government told him to stop; he refused. The abbé was arrested while preparing it for publication. Soldiers marched into the school and hauled him to prison.

"That's when Massieu saved Abbé Sicard's life," Pierrot told us one afternoon as we were finishing printing a journal for teachers.

We stopped cleaning the press to watch Pierrot tell the tale.

"It was during the Terror," Pierrot remembered, "when priests and royalists were killed, hundreds of them, their heads chopped off by the guillotine. Every day, we'd watch the carts, filled with people sentenced to death, roll by the school."

Everyone in the school was terrified by Abbé Sicard's arrest.

"Of course, they didn't worry about the abbé dying," Pierrot comented. "They worried about themselves.

"Only Massieu dared to speak out. The others were afraid that, if they defended Abbé Sicard, they would be arrested, too. Maybe even killed."

Massieu, who was watching him tell the story, had been silent. Now his eyes widened at the truth of Pierrot's words. He interrupted.

"I didn't want our dear abbé to die," he stated. "I was so upset, I couldn't sleep or eat."

He petitioned the government, this time for Abbé Sicard's release. He carried the petition to the National Assembly himself.

The lawmakers let Massieu present his petition. With the aid of an interpreter, who had deaf parents, Massieu presented it.

"It said," Pierrot's words slowed as he tried to remember. "Please free this man who helps the deaf . . ."

But Massieu, who had memorized the wording he had written, couldn't bear to see Pierrot distort and abbreviate it.

"It said—," he broke in. His signing became formal, in French word order, as he recited the words he had written so long ago.

"The students of Abbé Sicard have come to beg the return of their father, friend, and teacher. He has wronged no one, he has helped many, he has taught us to love the sacred principles of liberty and equality. He loves all men, good and evil."

Massieu stopped and his glance fell on Pierrot, who continued the tale.

"Everyone stared at Massieu," Pierrot signed. "Some people with their mouths hanging open . . ."

Massieu laughed. "They had never seen a deaf man before."

I imagined the gentle Massieu, not speaking, but warming everyone with his saintly countenance and elegant words.

Pierrot finished the story.

"When he was finished, they came up and shook his hand."

"They looked at me as if I were a priest," Massieu laughed.

Massieu always had looked like a priest to me. His eyes were kind and intelligent. Yet they always seemed to be looking beyond.

"Then you found the abbé in his jail cell," added Pierrot, proud to know the whole story.

"We held each other and cried," Massieu told us. "I tried to tell him how much we missed him and how much we loved him. We suffered so much thinking that he might die."

Pierrot's face took on a mischievous look.

"I'll bet he understood nothing," he prompted. His smile said he was teasing, but his emphatic gestures said he was telling the truth.

"He understood my feeling," insisted Massieu. "All of the prisoners who watched us understood."

I was afraid that Pierrot would anger him, so I broke in. "Then you freed him from jail?"

"No," answered Massieu. "Unfortunately, he stayed in jail. The government gave an order to free him, but in the confusion no one obeyed it—"

"No one obeyed the government?" I interrupted. I couldn't understand that.

"It was a revolution!" Pierrot was impatient with me. "The king was in prison, people were dying every day. Everyone was scared that they would die next."

"It's hard to imagine now," Massieu consoled gently.

"They killed many priests," continued Pierrot. "They probably didn't kill Abbé Sicard because Massieu had named him—" (he stopped for maximum effect) "the Father of the Deaf."

"He is our father," Massieu declared. "Our earthly father."

"They kept him in jail for days," Pierrot told us.

And much worse.

While Sicard languished in jail, Massieu pressed for his release, and the school, as well as the nation, drifted leaderless. Then France was invaded.

"The kings and princes of Europe were upset about the arrest of a king," explained Massieu. "They knew that if French subjects—remember we were not citizens then, but 'subjects'—could overthrow their rulers, their own subjects might do so, too."

"They wanted a king back on the French throne and they sent their armies to put one there." Pierrot still seemed angry at the thought. "While Abbé Sicard was in jail, foreign soldiers fought their way through the countryside toward Paris."

In turmoil, the French government decided to move their prisoners to a different jail. They were afraid that the prisoners would help the invading soldiers. The citizens of Paris learned about the transfer of the prisoners and gathered along the proposed route.

"Everyone thought they were spies," Pierrot explained.

Massieu nodded. "Traitors and spies."

The prisoners were forced into carriages and the jailers refused to close the doors. As the carriages lumbered across the city, the Parisians ran alongside, and tried to kill the prisoners by thrusting swords, sabers, sticks, stones, and pikes through the open doorways.

I was appalled.

"They cried, 'Death to the traitors and spies,' " remembered Pierrot, looking at Massieu for confirmation. Massieu nodded his head in agreement.

When Abbé Sicard's carriage arrived at the new jail, he was bloody from stab wounds. But his terror was not over. The crowd had followed the carriage into the jail's courtyard, all the while trying to stab the men inside it. There were six men in Abbé Sicard's carriage. As each man left the carriage and ran toward the prison, the crowd gathered round and stabbed him to death.

"Only Abbé Sicard, hovering in the back of the carriage, and the last man to leave it, made it inside the building safely," Pierrot went on. "By the time he poked his head through the carriage door, the mob had moved onto the next carriage."

Abbé Sicard ran inside the building, but he was far from safe. Some men in the crowd ran after him. As he entered a room filled with the jail's administrators, the crowd burst through the doors behind him.

Abbé Sicard thought that his life was about to end. He gave his watch to one of the administrators and asked that it be given to the first deaf man who asked for him.

"He knew that would be me," commented Massieu, overwhelmed at the memory.

"Then he crossed himself and prayed. He was ready to die."

Angrily, the crowd accosted him, sabers raised. Then, a miracle.

"You know Monsieur Monnet, the watchmaker?" Pierrot asked.

"With the fat wife?" asked Claude.

"Yes," Pierrot answered. "He recognized Abbé Sicard. Probably because of Massieu." He gestured toward the teacher, who was often in Monnet's store, looking at watches.

"Monsieur Monnet threw himself across the abbé's body, protecting it with his own," continued Pierrot. "Then he tore open his shirt and bared his chest to the mob, and cried—"

"He cried that they must kill him before they killed the Father of the Deaf!" interrupted Massieu, who had heard the story from both men, and would never forget it.

I was impressed. The crowd had been impressed, too. Soon they were all shouting, "Spare Abbé Sicard! Spare Abbé Sicard!"

"They would have carried Abbé Sicard back to the school in triumph," exclaimed Pierrot. "He would have entered the gates like a hero."

"But he refused," Massieu stated. "The crowd's clamor meant nothing. Abbé Sicard cared only about God—and the king—and orders from the official French government."

So Abbé Sicard had stayed in the jail all night, listening to wounded prisoners as they cried and moaned. In the morning, there were thousands of bodies in the courtyard.

But Abbé Sicard was freed. Before he came back to the school, he marched right back to the government that arrested him and made a grand speech of thanks.

"He'd only been back at the school a short time, when the government wanted to arrest him again." Massieu shook his head. "This time he didn't wait for the soldiers to show up in his classroom. He fled. He's been in hiding ever since."

I couldn't believe that Monsieur Monnet, the grizzled, old man whose wife yelled at him, was in that murdering crowd. I'd visited his shop with Massieu. It was hard to imagine those gnarled fingers, so good with the little wheels inside watches, wielding a sword against other Frenchmen, even if they were prisoners, and murdering them. It seemed to me that even though he had saved Abbé Sicard's life, it was only because he knew him and Massieu. How could he have killed other people?

"Monsieur Monnet was in that crowd?" I asked.

Massieu and Pierrot ignored me and I repeated my question.

Finally Massieu turned to me. His look of pain at recounting that time deepened.

"Everyone in Paris was in that crowd," he explained gently.

Since then, I had pictured Abbé Sicard as a kind of knight, saintly and brave. It wouldn't have surprised me if he had light around his head like the saints in the paintings in the chapel.

I learned more about people that day, as I watched Abbé Sicard embrace his excited student, Jean Massieu. How could such a man be so famous? I wondered. How could Massieu be so excited about him? I could not shake the questions from my head.

Then Massieu beckoned me and I rose to put a poem I had written honoring Napoléon, the leader of France, on the slate board in the assembly room.

As I printed the poem in careful large letters, I also hoped that Napoléon would end the fighting and killing, and bring peace to France.

Even Pierrot liked Napoléon, though grudgingly. He hoped, if Napoléon, or someone from the government, liked my poem, we would get more heat this winter.

As I finished, I stole a look at Abbé Sicard. He smiled, nodded, and gestured, in flamboyant approval.

Then one of the girls put a wreath on his head. As he sat in his chair, his medals sagged over his protruding paunch. He looked like a pagan god.

The audience applauded. I looked at the clapping hands and bowed. Then Abbé Sicard spoke. He moved his arms importantly as he talked. His signs were big and dramatic.

Something was wrong. I looked at Pierrot who was looking back at me. I was truly alarmed. I understood none of Abbé Sicard's signs.

Pierrot shook his head so very slightly. "I told you so," his look said.

My desperate eyes sought out Massieu. But Massieu, standing before his master, appeared content.

Abbé Sicard asked Massieu questions and Massieu responded. From Massieu's answers, I could guess Abbé Sicard's questions. But watching only Abbé Sicard, I was lost.

Eventually, I would come to understand Abbé Sicard. At that first meeting, I understood only that Pierrot was right. This man, the Father of the Deaf, could not sign.

9

Public Performances

The dormitory was still cold, but the school was more exciting with the return of Abbé Sicard. We started our performances for the public again. Twice a week, hundreds of people would roll up in carriages, enter the assembly hall with its sturdy wooden benches, and watch Sicard and his deaf students perform.

They called us miracles.

There is nothing more remarkable about teaching deaf children than hearing children. Abbé Sicard, though, encouraged his audiences to think that our learning was miraculous—and that he himself was a miracle worker. The performances helped bring money into the school. Abbé Sicard loved them.

I was often in the performances now. Massieu was still the star, but I had the best supporting role. It was often I who transcribed his signs into words, and wrote them on a huge slate board for the audience to read.

It was easy. Massieu would sign and fingerspell slowly in signed French. Knowing that one mistake would mean trouble for us all, he fingerspelled almost everything. I didn't have to understand what he said. I just had to transfer the flow of words from his fingers to the board.

As he answered questions from the people in the audience, Massieu continued to astound everyone with his brilliance and poetry.

I enjoyed the reflected glory. I was better at signed French now. Signed French was our classroom sign code for French—the dreaded classroom signs. It was different than the signs we used to talk with each other. To sign French—or English or any spoken language—a student takes signs from sign language and adapts them to the rules of French or another language. It is ugly and awkward. It is hard to understand, too. Our teachers required it.

Among ourselves, we used sign language. As far as I know, deaf people in Paris had used this sign language for a long time. Abbé de l'Epée, founder of our school, was smart enough to see it, learn it, and use it to teach deaf children in the classroom.

But he was not smart enough to leave it alone. It was our founder who was the first to put signs in the order of spoken French. To take a language based on sight and transform it into a code for a language based on sound was not easy. Nor was it easy to learn.

During my first years at the school, I hardly understood signed French at all, though I learned sign language fast. I didn't need French to transfer Massieu's careful signing and fingerspelling into print. I simply converted what he signed and fingerspelled, often letter by letter. It was a long time before I understood what I was writing.

"Signed French will help you learn French," our teachers said. I believed that for a long time.

Abbé Sicard didn't sign during the performances, except when he talked directly to us. I would never have known what he said, except that Pierrot's uncle told Pierrot about it.

His uncle came to the first performance where I was allowed onstage. I was so proud. It was good, I felt, for these people to come and see us. They would learn that deaf children were intelligent and caring human beings. My heart even softened toward Abbé Sicard. He must be a good man to bring our cause before the world.

First, Abbé Sicard asked Massieu questions. Then he encouraged people in the audience to ask questions. That way, they knew no one planned the questions and taught Massieu the answers. They experienced for themselves Massieu's spontaneity and his genius. I translated Massieu's responses into French and wrote them on the board for all to see.

A member of the British government was in our audience that day. "What is hope?" he asked.

"What is hope?" Abbé Sicard repeated the question and wrote it in large letters. Massieu read the question and answered it in careful signed French.

"Hope is the blossom of happiness." He finger-spelled every word except the first two. I wrote down each letter as he made it.

When I had finished, the men and women in the audience exchanged incredulous looks and broke into applause.

"What is gratitude?" asked a well-dressed woman.

Abbé Sicard wrote out the question.

"Gratitude is the memory of the heart," Massieu answered. I copied his signs and fingerspelling.

More looks of wonder were exchanged, then a new wave of hand clapping rippled through the audience.

"What is time?" asked a man in the back row.

"Time is a line that has two ends, a path that begins in the cradle and ends in the tomb," Massieu replied.

"What is the difference between desire and hope?" someone asked.

"Desire is a tree in leaf," answered Massieu. "Hope is a tree in bloom. Enjoyment is a tree with fruit."

Each answer brought a stunned moment of appreciation and surprise before applause swept through the watching crowd.

Such poetry. I marveled at my teacher even as I wrote his words on the board.

"What is God?" asked Abbé Sicard as a finale.

From his front row seat, Pierrot caught my eye on stage and shook his head. Napoléon wanted no talk of God, I knew. His wife, Josephine, was supporting a child in our school and she had once come for a visit. But the general never came. Pierrot believed that the more Abbé Sicard insisted on talking about God, the less our chances were for a visit from the great general.

"Guess we lost another allotment of coal," said Pierrot's contorted face.

I ignored him, keeping my eyes on Massieu. In the center of the stage, my teacher turned the question over thoughtfully. Finally, he answered.

"God is a necessary being, the sun of eternity, the mechanist of nature, the eye of justice, the watchmaker of the universe, the soul of the universe," he answered.

I could not remember all of that, and he knew it. He placed the commas himself and paused at each of them, so I could write each phrase.

I watched the applause that followed his response. People told me it was as loud as thunder.

Yet—despite my teacher's brilliant answers, despite the good opinions I knew were exchanged among those seated in the assembly hall—when Pierrot told me what his uncle had heard, I could never feel comfortable at the performances again.

"Abbé Sicard said we were savages," Pierrot told us flatly. "He said we were children with no thoughts, no feelings, no nothing. We were like statues until he, the great Abbé Sicard, woke us in his classroom."

Massieu had been called to Abbé Sicard's office to help with an emergency, the expelling of a student whose parents could no longer pay the school costs. As outspoken as he was, Pierrot was careful in his criticism of Abbé Sicard when Massieu was nearby.

With Massieu absent, he continued angrily, "He said that deafness doomed us to darkness and to hell. We are all children of the night. It is only through Abbé Sicard that we are saved."

"Perhaps he was just being dramatic," ventured Claude.

"He loves an audience," I added.

I don't know why I felt I had to defend him.

"You should have heard what he said when you came on the stage!" Pierrot turned angrily toward me.

His signs and face became pained as he imitated the abbé. I flushed in anticipation of his words.

"I want to introduce you to a new subject, almost an infant, a little savage, a block of unchiseled marble, a statue . . . brought to life . . ."

"He called Clerc a savage!" Claude was outraged. I was too upset to respond.

"A *little* savage," responded Pierrot.

My heart hardened. I, who had felt so proud, was suddenly ashamed. I had no more answers for Pierrot. I would defend Abbé Sicard no longer.

I had wanted to love Massieu's friend as Massieu himself did. Because of Massieu, I always treated Abbé Sicard with respect and courtesy. But he offended me.

He offended me because I felt that the man the world knew as the Father of the Deaf did not really like, or even know, us, his deaf students. Pierrot was right about his signing. He could only sign a little, and, except for performances when his sense of theatre called for drama, he threw his signs away. They were hasty, crippled spasms in his hands.

I have met other hearing people who work and live with deaf people and never learn to sign. Our language eludes them. They admit it. Abbé Sicard claimed that he knew signs well, as well as he knew "his deaf children."

In actuality, he was a stranger to both.

10

The Savage

I saw him first. Claude said he did. But, really, it was me. We were on our way to lunch and Claude was chatting about a new customer at the print shop, a rich man from Marseilles, when I noticed a group of strange men in the courtyard.

The men were well-dressed and had an air of purpose and importance about them. One of them held the end of a rope. At first, I thought the rope was attached to some kind of small animal, a dog perhaps, or a pig. As we got closer, I could see more clearly.

The form at the other end of the rope was a small human being.

I nudged Claude and, after a minute, he saw it, too. He stopped signing in the middle of a thought and his walk slowed. We got as near as we dared before we stopped and stared.

The human crouching in the men's midst was an ugly, white, naked boy. At least it looked like a boy. His body was shaped like ours, but his skin was whiter than cow's milk and hairless. His eyes were like an animal's, darting about the courtyard, as if looking for a way to escape. He was dirty and covered with scars. His knees were bent to his chest and he rocked himself back and forth without pause. Claude pointed at the yellow puddle on the earth beneath him. I looked and grimaced. It was urine.

Abbé Sicard entered the courtyard. When he saw the gathering, he extended his arms in his usual gesture of welcome. Obviously, the abbé had been expecting them, I thought. When he noticed the crouched form, he wilted like a flower. Abbé Sicard stopped in mid-stride, his smile fell from his face, and his arms drooped to his sides. He approached the men slowly, shook their hands quickly, and moved his mouth in tight, jerky movements.

He looked up and seemed to see Claude and me for the first time. We panicked, for we knew that boys are not allowed the curiosity of men. It was nosey and rude to stand quietly and watch the strange spectacle before us. We were supposed to be at lunch.

But the abbé didn't scold us. He had something else on his mind.

"Get Dr. Itard," his lips said. His hand motions followed the spoken command.

Claude didn't understand him, but somehow I did. Claude followed as I turned to go to the doctor's office. I almost bumped into our school's doctor. Dr. Itard was hurrying out of the main building, his eyes on the group of people in the center of the courtyard. Evidently, he had been expecting these people, too.

The men led the boy right past Claude and me as they entered the main building. We jumped back as they passed. The boy, using his arms and hands as well as his legs to walk, looked more fearsome close up.

We hurried to the dining room to find Massieu. He was the only person who could—or would—tell us the reasons behind what we had just witnessed. Massieu was not at lunch. He had gone into the city, one of the priests told us, perhaps to buy a watch.

We did not find Massieu until late afternoon. He was at his desk in the classroom, checking the work of the first-level boys.

The story tumbled out of us at the same time. Massieu watched one of us, then the other. He said nothing.

"You don't believe us!" I cried at last.

I was suddenly unsure of my memory. Had Claude and I truly seen a naked boy led by a rope by well-dressed men in our school courtyard?

Massieu still did not answer. Claude and I fidgeted restlessly as he ran his fingers through his long hair, checked his new watch for the time, and looked thoughtfully at the wall at the opposite end of the room.

"We saw a savage." Claude was firm and grave.

"His name is Victor." As usual, Massieu stunned us with his knowledge and acceptance of a situation that we found extraordinary.

Then Massieu asked a question. "Do you think he's deaf?"

I looked at Claude.

"Not deaf," Claude signed.

"Maybe hard-of-hearing," I compromised. Why else would they bring a child—if the savage were a child—to our school?

"Not hard-of-hearing," Claude responded surely.

I felt impatient. How could Claude know if that strange animal had use of his ears or not?

"Why did they bring that boy here then?" I asked him. Claude echoed my question.

"*Is* he a boy?" I persisted.

"You saw him," responded Massieu. "Did you think he was a boy?"

"He looked like a boy . . . but he also looked . . . like a small pig," I offered.

"He's a boy," stated Claude.

I'll never know where he got such sureness.

"People say that he's a boy who was raised by wolves," explained Massieu.

"Raised by wolves!" I was shocked.

"That's what they say," Massieu replied mildly.

Then he told us a fantastic story, a story that traveled around the world. The tale is still told in French, English, and dozens of other languages. In America, they called the boy the Wild Boy of Aveyron. In my school, we simply called him the Savage.

"They saw him first in the woods," Massieu told us. "He was naked and running with his hands as well as his feet. He was quick, too, like an animal.

"Somebody captured him. They chained him to a stake in the center of the village. People came from all around to see him. They stared at him and teased and tortured him, too. Finally, he broke loose and escaped back into the forest.

"A widow took him into her home," Massieu continued. "He wouldn't wear proper clothes, so the widow made him a gown of white linen.

"Perhaps he still wants to escape." Massieu rubbed his chin. "At the widow's house, he spent most of his time prowling around his sleeping room, looking for a way to get out.

"The boy chooses his food by smell and eats most foods raw," Massieu told us, "except potatoes. Apparently, he prefers his potatoes cooked black on the outside and still raw on the inside.

"The boy doesn't talk at all but makes animal noises. He's mute," Massieu told us, "like we are."

Claude and I couldn't understand what the boy had to do with us.

"He's not a deaf boy," Claude repeated.

"He's got a lot of scars," I remembered.

"Maybe from living in the woods," guessed Claude.

Massieu thought not. "I've heard that the biggest scar is on his neck," he sighed. "Someone tried to cut his throat. They wanted to kill him."

It seemed impossible for the horror I felt to intensify, but it did.

"Why did they bring him here?" I asked.

"His intelligence is locked up, like a deaf person's who doesn't know signs." Massieu shrugged. "The abbé is the best teacher in the world. Perhaps he can help him."

"The abbé himself will teach him?" I was aghast.

"That's stupid." Claude was firm.

Massieu smiled.

"Perhaps he'll be in your class," he suggested to Claude. "Perhaps he and I will talk philosophy one day. You can join us, if you've finished your reading."

He ruffled Claude's hair. We all laughed. We knew Massieu was teasing now. I doubt if Claude had even begun our reading assignment.

Massieu suddenly became serious. We were the students; he, the teacher.

"The questions are: Why is the savage boy, Victor, the way he is? Was he born that way or did he become that way? Would all of us be like Victor if we were abandoned and raised by wolves?"

Massieu paused. "Of course, the most important question is: Can we help him?"

I shuddered. I wondered what it would be like to have a wolf for a mother. Would Claude, or Massieu, or even Abbé Sicard be like the Savage if they were raised in the woods? Would I be like that?

The next day, Massieu observed the Savage himself.

"I don't think Victor's deaf," he told Claude and me. "I think something else is amiss."

He told us that it would be Dr. Itard, not Abbé Sicard, who would teach the boy. Dr. Itard actually had moved into an apartment at the school with the boy. He planned to work with him every day.

"Dr. Itard doesn't sign!" I protested.

"It doesn't matter." Claude was convinced. "The Savage is not deaf."

"Victor," corrected Massieu.

"It doesn't matter," Claude repeated.

"Dr. Itard is trying to teach Victor to speak," Massieu stated, ignoring Claude. Claude and I looked at each other.

"Put him in Abbé Magaron's class," I joked.

After that, my only knowledge of the Savage came from Massieu. "Progress is slow, deadly slow," he acknowledged one day in the print shop. "Victor has learned his name, though. He keeps his clothes on. But even dressed, there's no mistaking him for a Parisian boy."

"He helps our school get money maybe," I commented. I knew that the Savage had attracted the attention of all Paris. They were more fascinated by the savage boy than by the deaf boys.

Massieu nodded. "The same educated and wealthy men, the Society of the Observers of Man, who once interviewed me, now interview Victor," he stated. "Victor has made our school, and Dr. Itard and Abbé Sicard, even more famous."

Only Pierrot was spiteful. He felt that sending the Savage here was just another try to mix deaf people with crazy people.

"Abbé Sicard and Dr. Itard are such generous, dedicated men," he signed sarcastically, copying the gestures of the wealthy women who collected around Abbé Sicard after each performance. "Such wonderful men to help miserable people like the deaf and the Savage."

Then he returned to his normal demeanor. "Deaf. Crazy. We're all the same to them," he concluded.

But I was grateful to the savage boy. He kept Dr. Itard busy. While he tried to cure the crazy boy, Dr. Itard paid less attention to us. The Savage lived at our school for five years, the whole time I was a student. Finally, Dr. Itard gave up. The Savage was moved to the house of an older woman down the street.

I didn't like to see the savage boy leave. Now, Dr. Itard could spend more time trying to cure the deaf.

11

Doctor to the Deaf

From the beginning, I disliked and feared Dr. Itard. It was me, though, who brought him to our school. I had no choice.

It was right after Abbé Sicard had returned. Gazan, one of the younger students, tumbled down the stone stairs, steep and high, while rushing to dinner. Unconscious, he lay in a heap, his right leg twisted behind his back.

Seeing him, Pierrot and I ran for Massieu, each of us going in a different direction. Both of us ended up back at the foot of the stairs with the small crowd of students gathered around Gazan.

Massieu appeared just as we returned. Quickly, he turned to Pierrot and sent him for Abbé Sicard. Then he turned to me. Pulling a slim piece of paper from his pocket, he wrote out a brief message, and gave it to me.

"Clerc," he instructed urgently. "The hospital. Val de Grâce. Get a doctor. Go."

I nodded. I knew Val de Grâce. It was almost next door. We had gone there when anyone in our school needed medical help. I shoved down my hatred of doctors and my fear of the hospital.

Clutching the paper, I ran. I rushed into the hospital, afraid for Gazan's life.

I found myself in a large room, where men lay two in a bed, side by side. No air moved and I was grateful that I couldn't smell. I saw a man standing by one of the beds. I knew he was a doctor, maybe even a surgeon, because of the instruments he held in his hands. I walked up to him, pretending not to see his look of impatience, and shoved the note into his hands.

He read it quickly, even angrily. Then, putting away his instruments with appalling slowness, he made ready to follow me.

He seems earnest enough, I thought. But his eyes carried the coldness I remembered from the doctors of my childhood. As I tried to hurry him back to the school, I felt my old fear of doctors return. I was right to be fearful.

Gazan had recovered consciousness and Abbé Sicard had joined the group at the bottom of the stairs. The doctor found that Gazan's leg was broken. He set it and gave orders for him to be carried to bed and forced to stay there until the bones had healed.

Afterward, he and Abbé Sicard went into the abbé's office together. At the end of their conversation, our school had its own doctor. Dr. Itard was on the staff. He set up his office in an empty classroom, filled it with his medical books, charts, and even a skeleton that stood in the corner and stared vacantly at us when we were examined.

This doctor examined us many times. His name was Jean-Marc Itard and he was a surgeon. The Savage distracted him for a while, but soon he found time to begin experiments on us deaf boys.

Massieu's sign for Dr. Itard, which was quickly adopted by all the students, was the handshape "I", little finger pointing up, circling the ear very quickly.

"It's an 'I' because that's the first letter of his name," I explained to Allibert, a new day student from Paris who was sometimes a little slow in catching jokes that were clear to the rest of us.

Pierrot took over the explanation.

"It's near the ear because that's the only part of a deaf student that interests him. It circles quickly because that's the same motion as the sign for *crazy.*"

Allibert looked confused by our laughter.

"Dr. Itard wants to cure deafness," Claude tried to explain.

"And that's crazy," added Pierrot.

In the name of science, I was part of his experiments. What waste, folly, and pain.

The first time was when I was a student. It was almost funny.

Dr. Itard thought that, with special training, we deaf students could learn how to hear. He needed only to loosen our stiffened ears and make them work.

We marched into a special classroom and Dr. Itard marched in behind us, carrying an old drum—the Savage's, someone told me. After we were seated, he struck the drum with full force.

There were eight of us in the test group that day. We watched him whack the drum and trembled with him at its vibrations.

Dr. Itard never attempted to sign, and he was careful to bring an interpreter with him. The interpreter, a hearing priest, told us to raise our hands when we heard a noise. As the instrument struck the drum, eight hands shot swiftly into the air.

I have to admit I felt a bit pleased with myself, with all of us. There was not a deaf student in the class that day. No matter what instrument Dr. Itard used, we heard it. When he struck the drum, vibrations struck our ears.

"Only raise your hands if you hear noise," the interpreter said for the seventh time. "If you don't hear noise, don't raise your hand."

Then Dr. Itard would strike the drum, the vibrations would sweep the room, and eight hands would shoot quickly toward the ceiling.

Dr. Itard didn't look pleased, though. By the end of the class, his brows were knit together and his lips pressed so tightly together that his mouth had almost disappeared.

The next day, the eight of us returned to find that the drum had been moved from its position of honor in the front of the room. Dr. Itard stood with it in the back. Only the interpreter remained in the front of the classroom.

The priest asked us to be seated and face him. We were going to repeat the experiment, he signed, only this time our eyes were to remain on him in the front of the class; Dr. Itard would again bang the drum, but this time behind our backs. We were to raise our hands when we heard the noise.

At first, I was puzzled at this new configuration. What difference did it make where a boy put his eyes when listening was done with the ears?

I watched the interpreter and waited for the crash. It never came. I waited and waited. Finally, Allibert's hand ventured tentatively toward the ceiling. He started to turn toward Dr. Itard, but the interpreter stopped him.

"Did you hear the drum?" the interpreter asked him.

"I think so," he responded.

"Okay. Again," instructed the interpreter, and his eyes returned to Dr. Itard in the back of the room.

I watched the interpreter while the silent moments passed. Again, Allibert's hand rose. He looked embarrassed and tried to pull it down before the interpreter noticed him.

Too late. "Very good, Allibert," praised the interpreter.

Everyone except Allibert was sent back to class.

"Did he strike the drum?" I asked the interpreter as I walked toward Massieu's class.

"Twice," he answered.

I was amazed. The sensation I had had when I saw the drum struck had not occurred. It appeared that I only "heard" when I saw—and tried to hear. What I could not see, I could not "hear."

I encountered Pierrot heading toward Dr. Itard's classroom with a group of the senior boys.

"Worthless," he signed to me with a shake of his head as we passed in the hallway.

I laughed. I was happy to return to class. It was where I belonged and where I wanted to be.

At lunch, I learned that Allibert and Pierrot were two of the six boys in the whole school who actually had heard the drum.

Pierrot still seemed unsure.

"It didn't sound like a drum," claimed Pierrot, who had been able to hear until he had fallen sick when he was eight years old. "It was just a feeling in my head. I wouldn't have paid attention to it if I hadn't been sitting there in the classroom—trying deliberately to hear something."

Then Dr. Itard had modified the experiment. Instead of hitting the drum forcefully, he struck it lightly. Pierrot, still looking in the other direction, "heard" that, too. He had talked with the interpreter afterward and knew the details of his success.

Pierrot, who hated doctors more than he hated priests, and speech more than he hated French, began to go to speech class. Every day, he, Allibert, and four other students went to Dr. Itard's classroom to learn how to hear and talk.

"It's different than the speech class you took with Abbé Magaron," he told me often.

"Yes," agreed Claude. "It's four hours long."

Pierrot glared at him.

"Our class is scientific." He defended his position.

I gaped, Claude rolled his eyes.

"Dr. Itard is a doctor," Pierrot noted angrily. "He uses the rules of science to train us."

"What have you learned?" I was noncommittal.

"I can tell some sounds apart," he answered. "I can distinguish between vowel sounds and consonants."

"We did that with Abbé Magaron," I retorted, forgetting that I hadn't heard the difference, only seen it on the lips. "So what?"

A tiny part of me was jealous. It 's easy to want what you don't have, especially when your friend has it.

Dr. Itard soon weeded out three of his six students. Allibert survived the cut and so did Pierrot. Dr. Itard's class irked me. It irked Claude and most of the other students, too.

"I'm not deaf," Pierrot told us now. "I'm hard-of-hearing."

One day, when the subject of the savage boy came up in printing class and Pierrot complained, as he always did, that hearing people were always mixing deaf students and crazy people, Claude tried to tease him.

"We're all the same to them," Pierrot insisted for the hundredth time.

"We?" asked Claude gently, teasing Pierrot about his new-found status as a hard-of-hearing person.

"We," Pierrot repeated angrily.

Then he cut us to the bone. "People confuse hard-of-hearing people with those who are deaf and crazy," he signed, grinning.

"I'm only teasing!" he protested when we turned away.

To us, it wasn't funny. Claude refused to look at him, as did I. Massieu looked annoyed.

Pierrot blushed suddenly, and apologized.

Pierrot's stature as a hard-of-hearing person was short-lived. Dr. Itard gave up on all but one of his three hard-of-hearing students.

"He said we can't learn how to hear and talk because we sign too much," Pierrot reported. "He said we would have to give up signing completely to learn to talk."

Dr. Itard was going to take one of the boys into his home and demand that the boy use his voice.

"Who?" I asked, feeling a bit sorry for the boy.

"Allibert," he answered.

Of course. Allibert had never lived at the school; he only came for classes. He didn't sign all the time like the rest of us did.

"Poor guy," sympathized Claude.

Massieu was the only person to argue with Dr. Itard. Everyone else, believing in science, and perhaps hoping for a miraculous cure, supported his work. It puzzled me why Massieu was so opposed to Dr. Itard's experiments.

Massieu thought that Dr. Itard should treat our illnesses but leave our deafness alone. Dr. Itard thought that deafness itself was a sickness.

As Dr. Itard could not sign, Massieu wrote him notes. Doctor and teacher took turns erasing the other's position and scribbling their own on a slate.

"Deafness is a disease. You don't choose to be deaf," wrote Dr. Itard.

"Then poverty is a disease," wrote back Jean Massieu. "No one chooses to be poor. People can live without money and people can live without sound."

I didn't like doctors, and I disliked Dr. Itard. However, I tried to appreciate the importance of his science and explain it to Massieu.

"We aren't at school to be coddled," I told my teacher. "Perhaps Dr. Itard is right to experiment on us. If his experiments lead to a cure for deafness, it would be wonderful," I concluded.

"If he wants to cure us, why doesn't he like us as we are?" Massieu asked.

He had a good point.

We tried many of Dr. Itard's cures. First came the leeches. Itard put the slimy, black bloodsuckers on the ears of every student at St. Jacques. He tried to put them on my ears, too, but I told him that a doctor had already tried leeches on me. I told him that using leeches had not cured any deaf person I knew.

When the leeches didn't work, Dr. Itard moved on to electricity. Electricity was a new discovery, and Dr. Itard was one of the first people to use it to try to treat a human condition. He shot electrical current through our earlobes. First the skin would itch, then tingle, then burn. When we cried, Dr. Itard increased the current.

When Massieu protested, I defended the doctor.

"The pain isn't usually that bad," I lied. "He's not going to kill anyone."

Dr. Itard soon abandoned electricity as a cure for deafness. He had discovered a thin membrane, the eardrum, that, like a pulled window shade, interrupted the ear's passageway. Although hearing people, as well as deaf ones, have eardrums, Dr. Itard thought that in the deaf it might block noise and prevent hearing.

He set about surgically piercing our eardrums. Mostly it caused only excruciating pain, except in one of the younger students, Christian Dietz. After Dr. Itard had pierced Christian's eardrum some fluid escaped. Christian lay on his side in agony. He ran a high temperature and began to vomit. Dr. Itard was thrilled.

"The fluid, as well as the membrane itself, could have blocked the sound trying to flow to his ear," he wrote excitedly to Massieu. "Just give Dietz time," he continued. "Soon he will leave the sick room and have some hearing."

Dr. Itard was wrong.

"Christian's dead," Massieu announced without emotion after arriving late for class one morning. "Let us take a moment to say a prayer for his soul."

We prayed in stillness. Illness and death were as much a part of our lives at St. Jacques as the multiplication tables we memorized. In spite of its frequency, each time it felt new and terrible.

Claude, weeping, accepted some charcoal that Christian had stuffed under his bed. Christian's old books went to our school library and his uniform was altered to fit a new student. We celebrated a special mass.

One of the younger students asked Massieu if he thought Christian would hear in heaven. Massieu answered that in heaven we are neither deaf nor hearing. It was a good answer, I thought, though I didn't understand what Massieu meant any more than the eager boy who'd asked the question.

I know now that Christian's ears probably leaked fluid because they were infected. The infection eventually killed him.

Dr. Itard continued his search for a cure for deafness. He pierced the eardrums of five other students. They didn't die, but they didn't hear any better than Christian. So he searched for other cures.

He mounted a combination attack against deafness. He attacked deafness from the outside, peeling away the skin of the outer ear, and the inside, administering laxatives to remove from the body any loose deafness-causing agents.

Claudius Forestier, a student considerably younger than I, had the honor of receiving his attentions. Dr. Itard made Claudius drink strong laxatives. At the same time, he administered a bandage soaked in medicine to his ears. The medicine made the skin blister and peel. At thirteen years of age, Claudius had been an excellent student and athlete. Now he lay in bed, moaning and weeping. He only got up to relieve himself or have his bandage changed. He became so thin and weak, he finally couldn't get up at all and had to use a bedpan.

I joined Massieu in begging Dr. Itard to stop the treatments.

"If he's dead, he'll never hear," Massieu scribbled bluntly.

Only after Claudius stopped eating and became too weak to ask for the bedpan, or even cry, did Dr. Itard relent. After the treatments stopped, it was weeks before Claudius recovered enough strength to get out of bed.

Dr. Itard thought that perhaps Claudius's ears held a special resistance to his cure. He needed other students to learn if Claudius, and not the "cure," was the cause of failure. He tried the same combination of debilitating laxatives and blistering agents on thirty other St. Jacques students.

Nothing deterred the doctor, not the pain, the failure, the deaths. The experiments continued. It was no surprise to Massieu that all of the students were as deaf at the end of the experiments as they were at the beginning.

Using a hammer, Dr. Itard split open students's heads behind the ear. This would allow the sound to penetrate more directly, he reasoned, and perhaps circumvent the dysfunctional ear completely. He fractured several skulls with this treatment; he cured no one.

He also tried putting burning cylinders on the skin between the back of the neck and the chin. The treatment left deep scars, but restored no hearing.

Then Dr. Itard discovered the eustachian tube, the passage between the nose and the ear. He pierced the cartilage that separates the sinuses from these tubes in almost every student in the school. It took him almost a year.

I was almost twenty years old when he did it to me. It would be the last time I participated in one of Dr. Itard's experiments.

An assistant strapped me into a chair, clasping an iron band attached to the chair firmly around my head. My head was held back and my chin thrust toward the ceiling. I couldn't move.

Dr. Itard, his eyes fixed on my nose, walked toward me with a silver prong in his hand. No one had explained to me what would happen. Neither Dr. Itard nor his assistant attempted to communicate with me at all.

I knew what was coming, though, and squeezed my eyes shut. I felt the metal tip of the prong inside my nostril and then high inside my nose. Dr. Itard circled it upward and back, searching out my sinus cavities, pushing and breaking the sensitive tissue in an attempt to find the opening that led to the eustachian tube.

The pain was so intense, tears streamed down my immobile face. Nauseousness and lightheadedness overcame me. It seemed like an eternity before Itard wiggled the tool back through my nostrils and out of my nose.

It was over. He motioned me impatiently to get out of the chair and make my way for the next person. I tried to tell him I was dizzy and sick to my stomach. But the man had the skill of working on us without looking at us. My attempt to communicate was useless.

Resigned, I forced my body upward out of the chair, trying to turn away from the doctor at the same time. I threw up. My vomit landed on Dr. Itard's pants and shoes. I didn't look at his face, as he hadn't looked at mine. I hurried out of the room.

I returned seven times. Each time I cried and each time I vomited. Everyone did.

I stopped defending Dr. Itard to Massieu. In fact, I joined Massieu in criticizing him.

"Dr. Itard wants to cure deafness and be famous," I stated bluntly.

"He just wants to be famous," insisted Claude.

"He will be," predicted Massieu.

I laughed.

Massieu proved prophetic. After all the pain, the suffering, the violation of children in his care, how does the world know this man, Jean-Marc Itard? Torturer? No. Murderer? No.

Jean-Marc Itard is known as the Father of Ontology, founder of the science of speech and hearing, and bene-factor—yes, I've heard it often and read it also—bene-factor of the deaf. Which deaf?

None that I knew.

"Medicine doesn't work on the dead," Dr. Itard wrote as an old man. "As far as I am concerned the ear is dead in the deaf. There is nothing science can do about it."

What an enormous price we deaf at St. Jacques paid for his conclusion!

12

Reading More Than Words

I was a bit of a show-off, I guess. I was smart, and I knew it. Abbé Sicard told Massieu that I was one of the smartest students in the school. Massieu himself told me I was becoming a "gentleman." I had the highest grades in the class, perhaps because I read all the time.

Sometimes kids teased me, especially Pierrot. I had realized by this time, though, that Pierrot's impatience with French was at least in part because he did not know it very well. In spite of his classes in hearing and speech, he did not seem to be learning it, either.

For instance, when Abbé Sicard's godson Roch-Ambroise Bébian, a hearing boy living at our school, wrote him a note, Pierrot read it wrong. To Bébian's written question "How are you?", Pierrot answered "to room."

"I know why you said that," I told him importantly, "but it's the wrong answer."

"Shut up, Clerc," Pierrot answered without rancor.

I sighed. There was no talking with him about the French language and explaining that it was the French idiom that had led him astray. "How are you?" is an idiom in most languages, I think. I hate idioms, those confounding sets of words that say one thing and mean another, and fill every language, including my own sign language. Translated word for word into English, the question in French "How are you?", becomes "How go you?" One answers idiomatically "I go fine."

Pierrot had interpreted the idiom literally. He said he went to his room.

Bébian, who really seemed to like us and wanted to learn our sign language, became embarrassed and apologized. I was embarrassed, too, though I do not know why. Pierrot was older than I and he was my supervisor, but his French was worse than mine.

I was proud of my French and proud of my reading. I read earnestly and dutifully, more than any other student. I was often picked to read in class, and I easily converted the print to signs. I would sign exact French for Massieu and Abbé Sicard. I often read this way for our hearing visitors.

Of course, it was boring. I assumed that was how reading was supposed to be. I assumed that people read for the same reason they took foul-tasting medicines and ate bitter vegetables: it was painful, but it was good for you.

Massieu, though, never looked bored when he read. His face looked as if he were praying. He was relaxed, faraway, and yet, somehow, at home.

For me, print was a word-by-word struggle. I bought a dictionary with money my parents had sent me, and it was constantly by my side. Every word I didn't know, and there were many, I looked up. Sometimes, this meant looking up three or four words in each sentence. Sometimes, it meant taking an hour to read a page. Once, I tried to make my own dictionary, writing down every word that was new to me, and each of its definitions. Each word, it seemed, had many definitions. But the list became so long so fast, I stopped. There was not enough paper in the school, perhaps in the whole city, to accommodate my personal dictionary.

Often, instead of spending what money I had in a pastry shop, I would use it to buy a book. My parents sent me books, too. I kept them under my bed. I had more books under my bed than any other boy in the school.

I was proud of myself and my books, perhaps more proud than I should have been. Reading was more a tribute to my endurance than my curiosity or understanding. I didn't realize how little I understood.

I learned what reading really was through Pierrot and Massieu. They accidentally taught me this, my most important lesson.

Pierrot had given Françoise Deprès, one of the new female scholarship students, one of Claude's charcoal drawings. This was against the rules, but none of us cared. As we grew older, we passed more information to the girls across the streets than our teachers would ever imagine.

Claude was upset because Pierrot claimed the drawing as his own. Claude found Pierrot and me cleaning the press after a large printing job.

"You had no right!" he cried, knocking some wooden letters out of Pierrot's hands. "You are a thief!"

Claude was so furious that I was afraid he and Pierrot would get into a fist fight. I ran to the classrooms to get Massieu. He asked each boy to tell his story. As usual, he said nothing while they explained, letting each give an uninterrupted account of what had happened.

Then he turned to Pierrot. To our astonishment, he ignored the specific facts of the case before him. Massieu always worked on a level above everyone else.

Now it was as if the incident had not even happened. Massieu told Pierrot to leave the school.

"You're too old to stay here," he said.

Pierrot looked stricken, as though Massieu had slapped him.

"You graduated and took your first communion last year. You should give your place to another student. You should get a job. Then you can come back to the school and visit."

Pierrot turned white. Claude and I shared his shock. We had not expected this. Massieu, seeing the effect of his words, tried to soften them.

It was important for boys to grow up, he told Pierrot. It was important to leave school, to go out into the world.

"Have adventures," he urged. "Like Candide."

Pierrot shook his head, still unable to understand.

"Who's Candide?" I asked dully, to fill the empty space.

"You don't remember Candide?" asked Massieu, his face telling me that I should know him well.

I shook my head.

"He's in your book," he signed gently.

I continued to stare at him.

"Your book by Voltaire."

Again, I shook my head.

Without further comment, Massieu began the story.

Candide was a young, trusting boy, kicked out of his rightful home, who fought in the armies of kings he did not know against the armies of other kings he did not know. He made his way from Germany to Portugal, he suffered through an earthquake, and sailed the Atlantic Ocean to South America, where he sought after gold and treasure. Finally he returned to Europe, and married the woman he loved.

"He suffered," Massieu concluded, "but he learned about life."

We stared at him. Meant as a lesson for Pierrot, the story had proved exciting in its own right. Too bad books were not written in signs, I thought. Our sign language was truly the language of the heart. If a book could carry one-tenth of the life of Massieu's story, reading wouldn't be such a bore.

"Was Candide deaf?" asked Claude.

"Hearing," replied Massieu.

"C-A-N-D-I-D-E," he spelled the name again, looking at me. "It's the title of the book, too. By V-O-L-T-A-I-R-E."

He spelled the author's name twice, still watching my face. I couldn't understand why he thought I should know the story. I looked at him and shrugged.

"I thought you had read it," he commented.

"Not that book," I told him, "but I will."

It wasn't until he ambled over to his own stack of books, pulled one out, and held it up, that I felt an unwilling start of recognition. I knew that cover. It was one of the books under my bed. I had read it—twice.

But I had no memory of the tale of adventure that Massieu had just related. The block letters that I had been putting away spilled out of my hands onto the floor.

The attention switched from Pierrot to me. Both of our faces were white now.

"What's wrong?" asked Massieu. It was his turn to be puzzled.

I didn't answer. I couldn't focus my thoughts enough to try to comfort Pierrot or even to make myself pick up the wooden letters that lay on the floor.

"Your story and that book . . . the same?" I managed to ask.

Puzzled at my reaction, Massieu nodded and motioned me to pick up the fallen letters. I left the letters on the floor, and I stumbled out of the room.

My thoughts tumbled over each other. To me, *Candide* had been a tedious, muddled series of pages. It was nothing like the exciting adventure tale that Massieu had told. It was unrelated pieces; it was vague hints. Yet, Massieu had cited that book as his source. His information and mine came from the same place.

I didn't plan to go back to the dormitory. It was strictly forbidden during the daytime, unless we were sick. I went there anyway.

At my bedside, I bent down and pulled out the now-familiar book and peered again at its title and cover. Sweaty and a little shaky, I opened it. Almost reluctantly, I looked at the print.

I skimmed the first paragraphs, seeing Massieu's alive signs jump from the dead text. There were still many strange words. I didn't want to take the time to use my dictionary. I skipped the words that I didn't know. I didn't worry about how they hooked up with each other, either. I made no effort to find the right noun for the right verbs and forgot about Signed French. Abbé Sicard would have frowned mightily at my carelessness.

I read. I couldn't stop reading. As afternoon slipped into evening and the room grew dark, I struggled onward. I got a taper, lit the candle by my bed, and continued to read.

When it was noticed that I was not at dinner, Pierrot came to get me. I did not see him until he snatched away the book. Even then, it was hard to pay attention to him.

"Dinner," he signed.

I couldn't focus enough to answer. I reached for the book. Pierrot yanked it out of my reach.

"Dinner," he repeated. "Come now or miss it."

"I'll miss it," I told him, my eyes fastened on the book.

Finally, he gave it back to me. I don't remember seeing him leave. Nor do I remember seeing Massieu come in. Massieu never entered our sleeping quarters, but when Pierrot delivered the news that I preferred staying in bed to eating, he came up to check on me. Boys did not skip dinner in his experience, and he thought I might be ill.

He found me burrowed deep into my bed and even deeper into my book. He didn't interrupt and I was only aware later that he had stood at the entrance watching me.

I continued reading when the boys began to fill the beds after night study. By the time Pierrot indicated that lights had to be out, I had only a few pages left.

I undressed in the darkness, stunned at my discovery. What I had thought was reading really was not reading at all. The key to reading was not the thousands of words I didn't know, but the few words that I did know. My eyes had bumped along catching what I knew; my brain had filled in the rest. There were still plenty of mysterious words in that book. But I had understood it.

Books were correctly praised after all. In their own way, they were as magical as signs, as I had long ago suspected. Whatever I did with the book that night, I knew that it was what Massieu and Abbé Sicard meant when they used the word "read."

In my nightshirt, I recited my prayers in the signs of the deaf, crossed myself in the signs of the deaf and hearing, pulled the single blanket as high as it would go, and fell asleep.

A week later, Pierrot announced that he was leaving school. He was going to work for a friend of his father. He would drive his father's friend's carriage and keep it clean. He would earn twenty-two francs a month, more than half of what a hearing man would have earned. It was clearly a good job.

13

Holy Experiences

The pope, the holy father himself, was coming to our school. I was used to seeing famous people in our audiences. I was used to having princes and queens from all over Europe ask me questions. But the head of Christ's church on earth!

"Next, Christ himself will come," joked Pierrot, when he visited our school and learned the news.

Massieu was almost as excited as when Abbé Sicard had returned. Abbé Sicard was excited, too. At least, Massieu told us that he was. I never saw the abbé now. I was in the highest-level class, and he was supposed to be my teacher. However, he was rarely at St. Jacques. He was always away at important meetings.

A new dormitory was being built and, with the pope's promised visit, work on it was hurried. All the students were supposed to get new uniforms, too.

I tried to be interested in the pope's visit. I was pleased that the pope was coming, but it was not his visit that had me feeling so excited; it was not my coming graduation, either, or my approaching first communion. It was Françoise Deprès.

The only times I could see Françoise were at our twice weekly public performances, and the only time I could be close to her was at Sunday mass. Like Pierrot and Claude, and nearly every other boy at St. Jacques, I was in love with her.

I spent hours dreaming about her. I would watch the building across the street, where the girls slept and studied, and try to imagine what she might be doing. I imagined her watching me during our presentations. I was usually too busy—and scared—to look at her directly. I knew she watched me though; I could feel her eyes.

I could watch her more freely at mass. I would get to mass early, take my seat at the end of a row and bow my head. I would cover my forehead with my open hand, my fingers descending over my eyes in a kind of awning.

From the altar, I looked devout. But, behind my fanned-out fingers, my eyes would seek out Françoise, seated among the girls in the back on the other side of the chapel's narrow aisle.

I had only to control the lower half of my face. One tiny smile, and I was sure I would be condemned to hell.

Françoise always sat in the same place, next to the same girl, Marie Catherine. Marie was reverent, looking either at the priest or at her shoes. Françoise, my favorite, looked constantly around the chapel with her sparkling eyes, which came to rest frequently on me.

It was Pierrot who told me their names and their histories. Françoise and Marie Catherine were both scholarship students. Abbé Salvan, head of the girls' school, had tested them and brought them into the school. Françoise was not only a flirt, Abbé Salvan told Massieu who told Pierrot, she was also his smartest student. In fact, Pierrot said that she was maybe even too smart to be a girl.

I didn't mind her being smart. I minded a little that she was so bold and flirted with everyone. Pierrot related that Abbé Salvan, a gentle kindly priest, ignored her flirtatious behavior because she got such good grades.

I decided to ignore it, too. I loved her.

Longing looks communicate something, but not nearly enough. I decided to write Françoise a note and pass it to her as I left the chapel. I knew that she was bold enough to accept it, smart enough to read it, and maybe even in love enough to respond to it.

I wrote the first note during printing class, tore it up, and wrote another. I tore that one up, too. I simply was not sure exactly what to say. Finally, I settled on one sentence: "I like your bonnet."

The next day was Sunday and I arrived at the chapel, with the note hidden in the waistband of my trousers. My hands were wet and my heart was pounding. If the priests found my note I would be kicked out of school.

Perhaps it was my nervousness that made me late. I was forced to sit near the back, far from my usual seat near the altar. Françoise and Marie Catherine sat several rows in front of me. A large girl in a blue bonnet blocked my view of them. She didn't take her bonnet off until the final prayer.

I got up quickly after the prayer and stood in the aisle, letting the other boys brush past me. I thought about running up to her. My hand was poised at my waist, ready to draw out my secret message.

The girls began to file out. Marie Catherine was talking as they passed, but Françoise's eyes were looking for mine. As she passed, so close we almost touched, our eyes locked together for a moment. She was smiling, her lips parted slightly. I couldn't smile. I could only look at her, standing still in the aisle as the other students skirted around me.

It was wonderful.

Feeling the eyes of others on me, I permitted myself to flow along in the midst of the exiting girls. I was deep red and in glory.

The note remained tucked in my trousers. I had forgotten to give it to her.

Later, I apologized to God, or I tried to apologize. I couldn't quite guide my thoughts toward prayer. Françoise still filled them as completely as she had at chapel.

Concentrating in class was hard, too. I was nervous that my grades would slip. This was not the time to be distracted. I was at the top of my class in my senior year and about to make my first communion.

Communion was the real purpose of our years at school. Learning, for the sake of being able to communicate, was secondary; so was being able to get a job. For priests, all that was important was that our souls be saved. We had to learn in order to know about God and Jesus. We had to learn to know good from evil. We had to participate in the sacraments.

"Before God there is no deaf and hearing," the priests told us often. "There is only saved and damned. With communion, we are saved."

I knew I should be thrilled to graduate. I should be thrilled to be a saved soul equal to other saved souls. But it was only Françoise who thrilled me. Graduation might mean I would never see her again. I began to think about marriage.

The following week, I wrote another note. This time I would remember my purpose and give it to her. The note had the same one-line message; I signed it this time. At the bottom of the page, I wrote "Love, Laurent Clerc."

That Sunday found me no calmer than before. I arrived early and took my place in a front row by the altar. My heart beat wildly when the girls entered the chapel. Françoise and Marie Catherine were usually among the first to enter, but not this Sunday.

Marie Catherine was the last girl to come in. Françoise was nowhere to be seen. I forgot to hide my face. So great was my horror and confusion that I scanned the room openly, again and again. Marie Catherine, who usually greeted me with her eyes at least, kept her head bowed and stared at the floor. I noticed that she wiped her eyes several times with the back of her hand.

"She's crying," Claude, who knew how I felt about Françoise, was kneeling at my elbow, watching me watch Marie Catherine.

I didn't say anything, but her tears alarmed me. Françoise didn't come to chapel that day. Puzzled fear burned in me all week.

The following Sunday, Marie Catherine again entered the chapel alone. Her eyes met mine briefly, then she looked away.

I wished mightily for Pierrot. He surely would have known what had happened. As it was, I had no choice but to ask Massieu. For some reason, I felt shy asking him questions about girls. I thought about asking Claude to ask Massieu about it for me. But as soon as mass was over, I found myself walking next to him and the question popped off my fingers, seemingly of its own accord.

"Françoise . . ." I began. "What happened to Françoise . . . ?" I was too upset to spell out her last name. Massieu knew who I was talking about.

He looked at me a long moment before he answered. He picked his words carefully. I could see he did not want to hurt me. I could see he knew he would.

"Françoise was not a nice girl," he began. "She's pretty. She's smart," he explained. "But she's not a good girl."

I said nothing, just stared at him in disbelief.

"I hope God will forgive her," signed the wise Massieu. "It's better for all of us that she's no longer at the school."

I couldn't believe it.

"Where is she?" I managed to ask.

Abbé Sicard had sent her back to the house for poor people, where she had come from, Massieu told me. She would be looked after there, and cared for. Meanwhile another girl, a nice girl, would take her place in the school. Lots of deaf children waited to get in, I knew, and scholarships such as the one Françoise had were rare.

"Don't worry about her, Clerc," Massieu concluded. "She's not worthy of you."

Then he trudged off to his meeting with Abbé Sicard. The pope was coming the next day and final arrangements had to be made.

I hadn't cried for a long time and I didn't cry then. I walked angrily in no direction. I ended up in the courtyard, where the younger boys were playing tag.

I had Pierrot's job as monitor now, and I joined the game. I felt myself playing too hard, as if I were angry. When one of the students landed on the pavement because I kicked him by mistake, I apologized and quit the game. They did not want me to leave, of course, but I did. I was not setting a good example.

My memory of the pope's visit is flat, without excitement. He arrived the next day, flanked by a group of men, some of them in bright red clothes, all of them well-dressed and dignified.

I was part of the special performance for him, perched onstage with Massieu and Abbé Sicard. The pope handed Massieu a copy of the book, *Lives of the Popes*, and asked him to communicate in sign from it to me. This wasn't planned. Massieu and I, however, handled it easily. Massieu signed to me and I transcribed his perfectly signed French into perfectly written French.

I was good at signed French by then. It was as if a door had opened and I found myself in a new room. I knew I was one of the few students in the school who really understood both signed and printed French.

Sometimes, I even understood Abbé Sicard. He often spoke before he signed and I would catch what I could from his lips and what I could from his hands. Usually, I could make sense of the matter.

Of course, any of the students could have transcribed Massieu's signs. It was a silly exercise really, for human beings are far more than transcribing machines. Our gift is understanding; our gift is creativity. But no one seemed especially interested in that.

The pope, sitting on his throne, seemed astonished by Massieu and me. He was anxious to ask us questions.

Massieu answered the questions with his usual insight and clarity.

"What is hell?" asked the pope. Abbé Sicard wrote the question on the slate board.

"Hell is the eternal torment of the wicked," signed Massieu, as I transcribed his words on the board. "A limitless torrent of fire that God uses to punish those who die offending him."

Abbé Sicard, his medal-bedecked sash slouched over his ample lap, looked pleased. He nodded approvingly as I wrote down Massieu's words.

As I finished, I glanced at the audience. I saw Marie Catherine sitting among the girls. She was looking at me, too. Never brave, she acknowledged me nonetheless, shaking her head up and down ever so slightly, and curling the edges of her lips upward.

I understood. From the stage, next to Massieu, across from Abbé Sicard and the pope, I looked at her for an extra moment, and slightly shook my head in response.

I had begun a new friendship.

Marie Catherine never replaced Françoise in my soul. She never stole my being. Without her glowing friend next to her, though, Marie Catherine's quiet beauty became more apparent. Françoise smiled at all the boys. Marie Catherine smiled only at me.

I found myself thinking of her more and more. With surprising speed, I again thought about marriage. Marie would soon have communion and be saved. She was a good young woman. She would be a good wife.

Abbé Sicard summoned me to an appointment in his office. I felt sick. Perhaps he knew about Françoise and me, or perhaps he had seen the glances I exchanged with Marie Catherine, right in front of the pope.

I didn't sleep the night before I saw him. I was sure I would follow Françoise out of the school, a disgrace to myself and my parents, forever ignorant, forever damned.

And what about Marie Catherine? Had they caught her, too?

I hadn't been in Abbé Sicard's office since my entry into the school. Then Massieu had welcomed me, treating me kindly and with respect. Now the abbé was there, forbidding and formidable behind his enormous desk.

Exhausted from my sleepless night, I tried to hide my hands. My fingers were trembling.

"Clerc," signed Abbé Sicard abruptly in his crippled hasty signs, "do you like it here?"

"Yes," I could scarcely answer, so filled was I with horror, fear, and shame.

"What do you plan to do when you graduate?" he persisted.

Would this never end? I wished he would be done with it.

"Go home, Abbé," I signed humbly.

"I don't think you should go home, Clerc," he responded ominously.

So he had already told my mother. I couldn't even return home. I was not even good enough to live in La Balme. My eyes rested on him, pleading for forgiveness. Panic filled my soul.

"Clerc, we want you to stay here," he announced. "And teach."

I couldn't believe it! His face told me I was a bore and should leave; his signs told me to stay and teach.

"Clerc, you are smart. You have been a good monitor for the young students. You would make a good teacher in our school. You and Jean Massieu are our finest examples of what our school can do. I am offering you the post of teaching assistant."

"You want me to teach?" I still couldn't believe it.

The abbé swept into a discussion of my salary. My salary! They would pay me to stay at this school.

I left his office feeling dazed and wise. How I loved what I saw around me. I loved this school and its small community of teachers and students and the language of signs. I even loved the abbé. I thought about Marie Catherine. Perhaps she could stay, too. She could clean and sew. Perhaps we could have living quarters here at the school.

The graduation ceremony, where we took our first communion, was beautiful. After all the anxiety that had preceded it, the ritual itself was almost anticlimactic. I felt no different after eating the bread that Abbé Sicard changed into the body of Christ. But I enjoyed everything, especially watching Marie Catherine. She and the graduating girls recited a prayer in sign language. Abbé Salvan told us that they had written the prayer themselves. I thought that the girl I had come to think of as my future wife was the most graceful and beautiful of all.

We had a banquet after the ceremony. After it was over, Claude, myself, and the other senior boys planned to go into the city to continue our celebration. Massieu and some of the other deaf teachers and staff were coming with us. Pierrot would meet us, too.

We had gathered in the courtyard and were ready to go, when I realized that I had forgotten my money. I ran back to the dormitory to get it and happened to glance out of the window on the third floor. To my surprise I caught sight of Marie Catherine, accompanied by one of the women staff, walking down the street. I couldn't see her face because of the bonnet she wore, but I knew it was her. The bulky gray clothing did nothing to hide the youth and grace of her body.

I was elated to see her. Emboldened by our recent communion and Abbé Sicard's offer to let me teach, I waved to get her attention.

Marie Catherine didn't look up. Her head remained bent forward, her eyes on the pavement, as she walked past the window.

As I waved and watched, I noticed she carried a suitcase. My joy turned to horror as I realized what was happening. Marie Catherine, who had taken her first communion only that morning, who was now a soul equal to other souls, was headed toward the home for poor women—the same home where Françoise had been sent several months before.

Everything she owned was in her small suitcase. She would never return. I would never see her again.

From the corner of my eye, I noticed an unexpected movement and turned to see that Claude had come after me and was standing on the stairs, looking up at me.

"Hurry!" he signed. But when he saw the look on my face, he asked, "What's wrong?"

I couldn't answer and he climbed the stairs to be next to me. Together we watched Marie.

"It's wrong," I told him, pointing, too sick at heart to feel angry. I turned stiffly to get my money.

Everything I felt was for nothing, I realized. Nothing would change our destinies. Not Françoise's. Not Marie Catherine's. Not Claude's. Not mine.

I really didn't care anymore about our trip to the city. But Claude put his arm around my shoulders and we descended the stairs.

14

No Longer a Student

From my first day in the classroom, I knew I was born to teach deaf students. I loved the school where I had grown up and where I continued to live as well as work. Together, students and teachers made our own world, nestled in safety behind our school's walls.

We shared the hardship of winter and the joy of spring. We complained about the food, the administration, and the school's governing board. We whispered about Abbé Sicard's continued loyalty to the French royal family. When the lawmakers asked the dead king's brother, Louis XVI, to return to France and Napoléon to give up his power, we were overjoyed. We readied a special performance for France's new king.

We were growing, too. The new dormitory was finished and now we had almost one hundred students. The fame of our school had spread, and students came to us from around the world. From America, there was George Randolph, the son of Virginia landowners; from Russia, Alexander Machowitz, the son of a countess and, it was rumored, the Russian czar himself. My smartest student, Ferdinand Berthier, was from my own country.

Sometimes, I felt I loved them all—and I felt they loved me. They came, struggled, laughed, learned what they could, and left. It was a constant planting and harvest.

Although we discussed politics constantly and passionately, outside allegiances meant little within our
walls. When Napoléon and the French army invaded
Russia, we talked about it in class. But, as a teacher, I
talked about the French conquest without exulting in it,
in deference to my Russian student, Alexander.

And, when the French army limped out of Russia in de-
feat and humiliation, we talked about that, too. Throughout it all, Alexander was never the Russian enemy to
me, only my student. He never treated me as an enemy
either, only as his favorite teacher. We were a community.

Whenever Pierrot and Claude visited, they made
their envy apparent.

"You don't know what it's like out there," Claude
complained one afternoon.

He and Pierrot had stopped by the school at midday,
and I had invited them to stay and eat. They sat with
me, Massieu, and Bébian, a hearing supervisor.

"Most Frenchmen make Abbé Sicard look like a genius," admitted Pierrot. He rubbed his bread into his
plate for what seemed like the forty-seventh time. "And
there's always food here."

Pierrot and Claude thought that they were eating for
free. Secretly, though, I paid for their meals. Perhaps
the princes who applauded our performances could
have shared our food if they wanted. However, the
school's former students were no longer welcome. It
was a good rule, I thought. There was never enough
food for everyone.

"Clerc's written to complain about it," Bébian said
and signed.

Massieu's hands remained still. Claude and Pierrot
were shocked. No teacher had dared complain when
they had been students.

"About what?" asked Claude, looking at me.

"The food," I answered.

"To whom?" Pierrot demanded.

"To the school's governing board," I told them. "It does no good to complain to Abbé Sicard. He's old and no one listens to him anymore."

"And if you're fired . . . ?" Pierrot restrained himself from licking his knife.

"Where would Pierrot get a free meal?" Claude added, smiling.

I looked at Massieu for support. He offered none.

"I'm tired of it," I asserted, irritated with them as if it were their fault. "It's supposed to be part of my pay here, room and board. Sometimes the food is so bad, I can't eat it."

They looked at me in disbelief.

"Really!" I knew I must sound spoiled to them, but I didn't care. I was surprised at the depth of my own anger. "I have to spend my few salary dollars on other food. It's becoming worse and worse."

Massieu lowered his eyes and ate without comment.

Claude and Pierrot continued to stare at me. I knew why. Inside the school walls, deaf people ate poorly; outside the school walls, they starved.

Bébian tried to change the subject.

"Clerc's written the board before," he told Claude and Pierrot. "You were successful, too, weren't you? They pardoned those students?"

I knew he wanted me to cheer up.

"Yes, they let them take communion," I replied. I ignored Claude and Pierrot and spoke only to Bébian and Massieu.

"I couldn't see those boys leaving here unblessed— not after they had struggled hard for three years, only to break some silly—" I caught myself. "Only to break some not-so-important rules as seniors."

Bébian laughed at my hesitation. "You see," he commented to the others at the table. "Clerc's becoming quite outspoken."

"Lessons from you," signed Massieu softly.

I thought he meant Pierrot, but he was pointing to Bébian.

Like Pierrot, Bébian was too frank and too passionate. Like Pierrot, he encountered mostly scorn for his honesty and feeling. Like Dr. Itard, he wanted to change our lives. And like Dr. Itard, he failed. He suffered for the failure, too. I thought at first that maybe his hearing would save him. It didn't.

Massieu showed me how to succeed, Bébian showed me how to fail. Massieu, I copied. Bébian, though he was a man of strong convictions and bravery, showed me what not to do.

I couldn't help but respect Bébian—the way a person might respect a knight who had been wounded more than once by the same impenetrable foe. Bébian was an angry knight. He could never accept—or forgive—the way his pupils were despised and forgotten. Nor could he forgive the hypocrisy of the people who pretended to help us.

Roch-Ambroise Bébian was Abbé Sicard's godson. His parents lived outside of Paris and he had come to our school to live while he went to school nearby.

Bébian was an outstanding student, winning awards and fame for his studies. When he graduated, he could have worked anywhere. But he refused the many jobs offered him. He wanted to stay at the school. He would make his life's occupation working among the deaf. When his father tried to make him quit teaching because of his low rank and salary, Abbé Sicard promoted him to supervisor.

Abbé Sicard called Bébian the person who best understood his teaching method. He was one of the most caring teachers I ever knew, and the only hearing man who really learned our sign language.

But as he continued to teach, his ideas changed. He came to criticize Abbé Sicard's method. Worse, he expressed his criticism often and in public, and in a way that won him only enemies.

I was almost one of them.

We got along well at first. Two years younger than I, Bébian and I met when we were both students. He played ball with us in the courtyard and learned our signs quickly. In spite of the quick temper that accompanied his red hair, I enjoyed him.

But when he announced his decision to work at the school, he came to me to learn sign language. Then we began to argue.

I would show Bébian a sign and he would look at me as though I were playing a trick on him.

"That's not the real sign," he would tell me. "Show me what the sign really is."

"This is the real sign," I maintained, confused.

"It is not," protested Bébian.

"It is!" Why did he insist on arguing with me?

"Show me how deaf people really do it, Clerc." His signs held a plea.

I laughed.

"Deaf people only use certain signs in conversation," I explained. "We abbreviate to be quick, like the hearing do with spoken words."

He wasn't convinced.

"Learn the real signs first," I urged. "Then you can learn the abbreviated ones."

But he didn't care about the real signs. In fact, the signs I called "real," he called "fake."

"I used to hate those signs, too," I told him finally. I explained how I had called them "classroom signs."

I admitted that it had taken me a long time to understand those signs, but that they were the abbé's way of teaching deaf students.

"You'll be a teacher, so you must know them," I told him. "They are harder to learn, perhaps, but you already know French, so it will be much easier for you to learn signed French than for your students."

He flushed at that remark.

"Exactly," he snapped.

The more he learned, the more critical he became.

Although he was hearing and had only begun to teach deaf students, Bébian was ready to criticize the teaching of Abbé Sicard.

There was nothing gentle about his criticism either. As time went on, Bébian began to call the abbé's method, which had taken over fifty years to develop, a failure.

"It's hopeless," he told me almost angrily. "It's awkward. It's ugly. It doesn't work."

I was tired of arguing with him.

"And what would you have them do?" I asked.

"Deaf students should sign naturally," he said.

I felt a little angry. This hearing man would tell me how to teach deaf students.

"French is natural," I said.

He wouldn't listen.

"If a child hears, French is natural, if a child sees, signs are natural. If you can't hear, a hearing language on the hands is not natural."

He had an example.

"Are you writing a letter?" he wrote the question on the board in bold script.

"Say that in signs," he said.

Irritated, I did so, using careful classroom signs: *are*, present/formal/singular, four signs; *you*, formal/singular, three signs; *writing*, one sign; *a*, feminine/singular, two signs; *letter*, singular, two signs; *question mark*, one sign.

"Well, more than eleven signs," he counted.

"Thirteen," I pointed out that a separate sign was needed to show the singular use of the verb and the feminine nature of the modifier for the word "letter."

"Thirteen!" he repeated the word triumphantly.

"What's the point?" I asked.

"Sign it naturally," he told me.

I hesitated. Then for argument's sake, I did it, abbreviating the classroom signs. I had four signs: *you, write, letter, ?*

Bébian shook his head.

"You can do better," he quipped.

I began to lose my patience.

"First you criticize Abbé Sicard's teaching. Now you criticize my signs—"

Then Bébian, my student, used the knowledge he had picked up as the young boy who played with us deaf students. One hand became the paper, the other became the pen, his look became a question, and he directed it to me. His stance captured it. He was writing a letter.

"One sign." He was triumphant. "You can sign the whole question using one sign."

I couldn't help smiling. At least he enjoyed our signs and appreciated their efficacy and beauty.

"You look pretty deaf to me," I observed.

He smiled. "Thanks," he replied, seriously.

Bébian had an instant ally in Ferdinand Berthier, my brightest student, and perhaps the brightest student our school had ever known. Berthier was not very handsome, even as a child. He was smart, though, heartbreakingly smart.

"I want to be a genius like Clerc," he declared, when he was still in his first year here.

The remark made me shake my head, for I knew almost immediately that Berthier would surpass me, as I had surpassed Massieu. I hoped that, when the time came, I would be able to show as much gentleness and grace as had my former teacher and firm friend.

While I had struggled for three years to learn to read French, Berthier read, really read, everything he could get his hands on almost from his first day in school. He learned other languages, too, Latin, Greek, German, English.

"He's a genius," commented Massieu.

He was a gentleman, too. If Bébian had Berthier's manners and tact, perhaps he could change something here, I told both Bébian and Berthier more than once.

When the two of them talked about "natural signs," they scared me.

"Be careful," I warned them. "Some of the school's board members don't like signs at all. The best way to defend signs is as a representation of French."

Berthier refused to listen. He was reading about the French Revolution then, filled with ideas about liberty and the rights of man.

"We deaf have a right to our sign language," my student told me.

I was promoted to teaching the highest-level class. I would teach the seniors and prepare them to take communion. I wouldn't earn more money, but it was an honor and I was elated. It eased my growing restlessness.

Why I should have been promoted instead of Jean Massieu was not a mystery to me. Massieu had deferred to me almost from the time I started teaching. At first, it made me uncomfortable. Massieu had more than ten years seniority; Massieu was Abbé Sicard's special friend.

I had come to accept his deference. I loved my former teacher, but he embarrassed me a little now.

Massieu didn't pay attention to the obvious requirements of civilized society. He didn't care about dress, politeness, or manners. When a wealthy man took him to breakfast at a fine restaurant, Massieu dressed in purple velvet pants and a yellow-orange coat, and bedecked himself with half a dozen watches, most of which circled his waist. He chose to ignore the elegant breakfast food. Instead, happy to be free from what they served us at the St. Jacques, he ordered his favorite food, ham ("almost a whole pig," he told me), and a bottle of wine.

A little perplexed and perhaps amused, the man watched while Massieu ate with the speed of a starving man. He didn't offer to share his wine, drinking the entire bottle himself.

Massieu laughed uproariously as he told the story. I laughed, too. But I was glad I was not there. Especially when I heard that the man had complained to the abbé, who then had apologized for Massieu.

"You can't cure everything," Abbé Sicard told the man.

Massieu thought that was funny, too.

Nevertheless, the first time I saw him after my promotion, I felt embarrassed. I blushed at his greeting, as if I were ashamed. He knew about the promotion, of course, but he didn't acknowledge it. Instead, he told me the latest rumors. Massieu, always close to Abbé Sicard, knew everything. His words, more than the official communications of our administrators, were where we got our information.

Massieu told me that Baron Marie Joseph De Gérando, a wealthy hearing man who hated sign language, although he knew none of it, had joined the school's governing board.

"It's a pity," he remarked, with a sadness deeper than any I could remember. "He will probably become president of the board, too. He's very ambitious."

As he turned to go, he seemed to remember something. He turned back, shook my hand, and congratulated me on my promotion.

"You're an excellent teacher," he told me sincerely. "You deserve this placement. It will be good for our students."

"Thanks," I replied weakly.

I had underrated him. I had worried that he might be angry or jealous. I should have known better. Jean Massieu was a man without jealousy. He had little ambition and no false pride.

I had complained privately at my promotion because my salary had not changed. In all the years I worked at the school, I earned the same money as when I started. Massieu would be oblivious to this, too, I knew. He gave all his salary to Abbé Sicard for safekeeping, asking only for money as he needed it. He would be happy to live out his life as a well-loved teacher.

I wished I were like Massieu. I was not.

I had a need to do grand things.

15

"Deafness Is Nothing"

"Russia?!" Bébian signed the word as if it were an oath. "Clerc, why do you want to go to Russia?"

Massieu merely looked at me skeptically. But, as usual, Bébian did not pretend courtesy.

"You're not thinking clearly!" he exclaimed, shaking his head.

Massieu had brought us news that Abbé Sicard was sending a teacher to Russia to start a school for deaf students. My student Alexander's father (by now we were all convinced that Czar Alexander I was, indeed, the boy's father) had requested it. Supposedly hearing-impaired like his unrecognized son, Czar Alexander was supposed to be an enlightened ruler who wanted to bring learning to his backward country.

"Abbé Sicard has selected Jean Baptist Jauffret," Massieu announced. Surprised at my own boldness, I told everyone that I wanted to go with Jauffret.

"Russia is supposed to be a terrible place," argued Massieu. "Starving people, horrible winters . . ."

"No cafés," added Bébian.

"Learning is as important to the Russian deaf people as it is to the French deaf," I told them.

"How can you sign if your fingers freeze?" asked Bébian.

126

Massieu guffawed. I stared at both of them. It was clear that they did not understand at all.

Convinced of the justness of my cause, I went to see Abbé Sicard personally. I asked him to send me with Jauffret. The abbé looked as surprised as Bébian and Massieu had at the suggestion. He looked amused, too. I tried to explain my sense of mission and urgency.

"You've no need for me here," I told him. "You have Jean Massieu. The Russian deaf have no one. Let me go with Jauffret."

Abbé Sicard, like Bébian and Massieu, tried to discourage me. I was insistent. The abbé ended up promising to ask the Russians if they might accept two teachers. He would let me know as soon as he found out, he assured me.

It was weeks before Abbé Sicard summoned me to his office again. At first, I thought that approval had arrived from Russia and I should get ready to make a long trip. But as soon as I saw the abbé's face, I knew that my request had been denied.

The abbé's face was red and unsmiling. Something must be very wrong, I thought. I couldn't understand why denying me would require so much emotion.

I was unprepared for his explosion.

"Why do you betray me?" he cried after I sat down before his desk.

Startled, I could only stare at him and wonder if I had understood his question correctly.

"I will not put up with your sabotage!" he exclaimed, rising from his seat, and moving toward me.

In disbelief, I continued to watch while he berated me. His hasty crippled signs only gave me hints of what he was trying to say. But, as the signs arranged and rearranged themselves, there was no mistaking the abbé's meaning. He was accusing me of corrupting his teaching and spreading lies.

Dumbfounded and dazed, I finally regained use of my hands.

"Why do you say that?" I asked.

I did not stop with the question. I had recovered enough from the shock of his attack to deny it.

"I would never do anything to corrupt your teaching!" I was more than a bit outraged myself. "I owe my education to it. I owe my livelihood to it. For me, your method is successful. More than successful. For me, your method is sacred!"

He must have seen that I told the truth. He seemed to wilt before my eyes, his shoulders sagging and his body seeming to collapse in on itself, like it held no more air. Almost seventy years old now, he was less the head of our school, and he knew it. He also knew that I was telling him the heartfelt truth.

He said nothing.

"Who told you I criticized you?" I asked.

"No one," he answered slowly. "I just had to be sure."

I could only stare at him.

"Bébian came in to talk with me yesterday," he signed finally. "I always thought that he understood my teaching method better than anyone. He was very critical."

Bébian. Of course.

The abbé continued. "Bébian wanted to know if he could use your students and see what happened if they had some time to use 'natural signs' and 'natural sign language' in your classroom."

I sighed.

"He's asked me about that before," I told the abbé. "I told him that I didn't like the idea because we have so much work to do and so little time to do it. I don't like to depart from the lessons—"

"You told him no?" Abbé Sicard's brows rose high in his forehead and he looked pleased.

I had never lied to him and I was not going to start now. "I told him that I'd think about it," I answered. "I don't know why he came to you."

"Think about it!" the abbé's face grew red again.

"It would be an experiment," I explained. "Bébian wants to see if French can be learned better using 'natural signs'."

The abbé watched my face.

"Clerc, Bébian is playing with fire," he stated. "New people on our school's board don't like signs—any signs. Ever since De Gérando has joined the board, they talk more and more about teaching deaf students through speech."

I nodded. Strange as it may seem, there are people who believe that the best way for deaf people to communicate is through the speech we can't hear. These people detest signs—perhaps because they don't understand them.

"If they hear Bébian's talk about 'natural signs', and learn that he means those quick movements you deaf use when you talk to each other—" Abbé Sicard frowned. "Sign language would be finished in this school forever. De Gérando will tie our hands, literally."

I nodded again. "The best way to defend sign language is as 'French on the hands'," I noted. "It's a lot more than that of course, but the hearing don't understand that."

It was Abbé Sicard's turn to nod.

"That's my gift to deaf students," he asserted, misunderstanding entirely what I tried to tell him.

I started to respond, but he cut me off.

"Talk with Bébian," he pleaded. "He has the highest respect for you. He says you taught him everything. Convince him to return to the one true way to teach deaf students."

I promised I would, though I didn't think it would do any good.

"He says you taught him everything," Abbé Sicard repeated. "He'll listen to you."

Then he dismissed me, without even a handshake, merely turning his back to me, returning to his desk, and bowing his head over the papers that overflowed on it.

At the door, I turned as if I suddenly had remembered something. I paused and waited for him to notice me. Finally, he looked up.

"Abbé, about the trip to Russia . . ." I began tentatively.

He looked annoyed.

"Will I be able to go with Jauffret?" I finished.

"No." He shook his head. "Russia's a poor country. They only have enough money for one teacher."

He bent his head and returned to his work.

I closed the door carefully as I left his office. I didn't want him to know how angry I was.

I found Bébian in my classroom. He glanced up immediately as I walked in.

"What's wrong?" he asked, alarmed by the look on my face.

"You!" I told him. "*You* are what's wrong!"

I walked back and forth as I told him of my conversation with the abbé.

"The abbé blames me for your love of 'natural sign language.' He's furious."

I was unprepared for his response. Bébian burst out laughing.

"Clerc, you should be honored," he declared, "and I should be insulted. The abbé gives me no credit at all. Must all my ideas be attributed to you?"

I was even more angry when I saw his laughter.

"You don't know what you're doing," I told him. "It's not so much the problem you caused me with the abbé. That's straightened out. That's not what bothers me.

"What I don't understand is why you criticize his teaching before everyone. How can you? Can't you see what it has done for us? Can't you see what it has done for me?"

He tried to answer, but I would not let him.

"You place the whole school in danger with your constant complaints. Abbé Sicard told me the same thing that Massieu has told us. De Gérando—that hearing man who hates signs—has joined the board and he'll probably soon become its head. He's talking about teaching the deaf through speech. We must be careful. Hearing people like to think that signs are only a code for their speech. You'll have us all reading lips and trying to talk. Then you'll see what real problems are for deaf people!"

Always emotional, Bébian had turned deep red.

"His method did nothing for you," he told me impatiently. "You learned in spite of it, not because of it. Methodical signing is a waste of time—and intelligence."

Methodical signing. Signing by method.

"I talk with my students in sign language. I teach them in signed French," I tried to explain, aware that my signing was changing now, even as we talked, becoming more formal. "How else are we supposed to learn spoken French?"

"Deaf students would learn French faster if we let them sign naturally," insisted Bébian angrily. "As to those pompous ignoramuses who enrich themselves at our expense by sitting on our governing board, they can all go to hell—each and every one—for all I care."

There was nothing more to say. He was as red as the bricks in the wall, and it was a wall I was talking to. I tried to turn away, but, ever impetuous, he held me back.

"Clerc, you've taught me everything I know," he went on. "In class, out of class. You have a way of talking with people. I know if you approve of your students trying natural signs, the abbé will let me try it. I need your help. Just as an experiment. Just to see."

I looked at him a long moment.

My feeling about Abbé Sicard's methods—the method with which I myself had become a literate person—was very positive. But I couldn't question Bébian's sincerity. And no one could pretend that we had discovered all there was to know about teaching deaf students.

"I'll think about it," I told him, as I had before.

As I left the building, I saw Massieu, who had probably known all along that I wouldn't go to Russia. He must have learned that I had finally been informed, too.

"Better here, Clerc," he told me gently.

"Journeys are for the hearing," I was surprised at how bitter I felt.

He lifted his brows and nodded, no outrage or anger, just acceptance.

"If only one person could go, then that person should have been you," he consoled me. "You do what Jauffret does, only better. You also do what he can never do. You prove that the abbé's method is a success."

"As do you . . . as does every educated deaf person. So why do they educate us if they don't want us to use our education?"

"Our souls," he began, but when I recoiled, he smiled.

"It's no crime to be deaf," he reminded me gently. "Remember Berthier?"

Our brightest student had been a recent recipient of a Dr. Itard's latest "cure." Dr. Itard had punctured his eardrums. Berthier had sweats, nausea, fever, and lots of pain—but no hearing.

"Are you disappointed?" Massieu had asked him gently as the fever abated.

"Not at all," responded our best student, weak from his ordeal, but strong despite it all. "I'm used to being deaf. There's nothing wrong with it."

"Nothing," I made the sign, flicking my fingers outward into emptiness. Deafness is nothing. What makes me so angry are hearing people. Abbé Sicard, Jauffret, the Russian czar. People infuriate me."

"The hardest part of being deaf is the attitude of the hearing," agreed Massieu.

A feeling of injustice gnawed at me all the time now. To be deaf is to live with injustice. People who should know were particularly unjust—people who said they were helping us.

I tried to work against the mentality that imprisoned us. I wrote letters of protest to the board. I wrote to protest the practice of confining deaf women in asylums and poor houses to live out their lives.

I was growing bitter at St. Jacques. I was almost thirty years old and had taught there for almost ten years. Never once had they increased my salary. The food was vile. Even the students, our purpose and our joy, disappointed me sometimes. Bébian was right; we had no sure way to teach them. With exceptions, I even sometimes felt that my teaching was accomplishing nothing.

Usually I hid my feelings, especially from my students. I owed them my best, and I always found energy to be cheerful and correct in the performances and in the classroom. No matter what, it was important that money keep coming into the school. No matter what, it was important that the deaf children of France have a chance to learn.

Massieu broke into my thoughts. "You are coming with the abbé and me to England."

"England?!" I was not prepared for that.

Massieu was grinning now. He knew of my restlessness; he knew I would be pleased.

"Haven't you read the papers? Napoléon's escaped from prison. He's gathered another army and he's marching to Paris. Perhaps we will not have a king much longer. The abbé thinks we should leave for a while."

Of course, I read the papers. Everyone in France knew that our famous general was on his way back to Paris, winning battles and slaying the king's soldiers as he came. As Abbé Sicard's loyalty to the king was well known, and the king himself had come often to our performances and met personally with Massieu and myself, none of us were pleased with Napoléon's advance.

"When do we leave?" I managed to ask.

"Next week," he replied.

I was thrilled. I knew my life was about to change. But I did not know by how much.

16

Why Can't the English . . . ?

London was a disappointment. It was not as pretty as Paris; the people were more restrained and the streets, just as dirty. The food was horrible, too. Bad wine, boiled meats and potatoes, lousy bread. No cheese.

Massieu's and my best entertainment was Abbé Sicard. Surrounded by people who spoke a language very different from his, our dear abbé was completely at a loss. Massieu and I had no trouble getting around. We were used to feeling separation from those around us.

Further, we knew how to use our bodies to ask for things. One doesn't need words in a bake shop to buy bread. One merely gets the owner's attention, points to the loaf of bread one desires, and smiles and nods "thanks" when it is given.

Abbé Sicard didn't know this. He was much disconcerted. What seemed to bother him most was the unwillingness of the English people to speak to him in French. The simplest tasks—ordering food in restaurants, purchasing bread, paying for lodging—upset him.

"Our abbé has lost his air of self-importance and control," I observed to Massieu.

Yet, Abbé Sicard criticized the language he didn't know and complained about me spending time studying it.

"It sounds so rough," Abbé Sicard told me one day, as the two of us finished breakfast in our hotel.

I told him that the sound of it meant nothing to me.

He glanced over at two Englishwomen next to us, their faces pink, their mouths moving excitedly. "They can't possibly be saying anything truly important," commented the abbé.

Nevertheless, he constantly asked our interpreter to translate conversations. Worse, he was never satisfied with the poor man's translation. Either the translator's reports were too short, or they were too long, or they were inconsequential.

When the interpreter condensed a waiter's lengthy discourse on what was available that evening into two words ("mutton or beef"), the abbé threatened to fire him.

Abbé Sicard's nervousness intensified after we got lost. It happened as the abbé, Massieu, and I were on the way to our first performance; we were tense, and anxious to see how the English public would accept us. Tickets to our performance had been sold out. English nobility, we had been told, had bought the majority of them. Members of Parliament, dukes and duchesses, and high-ranking members of the English church would be there, too.

The theater was a short walk from the hotel and we had already visited it earlier in the day. We had no doubts about finding it, and to this day, I don't know how we missed it.

Our interpreter had gone before us to make sure that the room was ready. Abbé Sicard, Massieu, and I left together, the abbé in front and Massieu and I following. We had wandered quite a distance and rounded several blocks before Massieu and I suspected that something was wrong.

The abbé's pace quickened and the crease between his brows deepened. He jerked his head back and forth as he tried to look in all directions at once. When his nervousness became panic, he turned to Massieu. Guessing that he was as lost as we, Massieu didn't wait for him to explain.

He handed over the announcement that explained our presentation; the address was printed on it. Massieu pointed to a group of English people.

"Ask them," he suggested.

Abbé Sicard looked from the announcement to Massieu and me, to the group of people, back to the announcement, and back to us. Then, waving the announcement before him, he marched up to the English strangers.

Massieu and I watched as they gathered around him, a mixture of amusement, curiosity, and helpfulness in their faces. They exchanged lots of mouth movements, points, and hand waves. I glanced at Massieu, who seemed proud of his friend.

Abbé Sicard, bowing slightly as he backed away, moved his mouth at the same time. The English twittered. I looked at Massieu for an explanation.

"He probably tried to use his English to say 'thank you,' " Massieu explained. "French hearing people can't say the English 'th'."

Coming abreast of us, Abbé Sicard scoffed, "They have such a primitive language."

As the strangers walked away, Massieu and I nodded our thanks in their direction, and they returned our nod. Then we looked hopefully at the abbé. He stared back.

"I understood nothing!" he exclaimed.

He turned on his heel and Massieu and I followed him. We walked twice as fast now; but to where we didn't know. Intent on following Abbé Sicard, I had not myself paid attention to the direction. Now all the streets looked alike.

The abbé turned around again. He began to scold us for being late! It was a very serious matter, he told us. We had to find either the theater, or the hotel, or a cab immediately. Startled, Massieu and I fell into step behind him and the three of us marched onward.

Abbé Sicard saw another man and practically ran to him, the announcement outstretched in his hand. He didn't try to talk this time, merely pointed to the address. The Englishman made rapid mouth movements and gestures. The abbé watched helplessly.

"What do you think he's saying?" I asked Massieu.

"Perhaps he's explaining the Pythagorean theorem," replied Massieu.

I realized that, without underestimating the seriousness of the problem, Massieu was starting to find the situation funny.

"Do you think we'll ever find the hotel again?" I asked playfully, catching his mood.

"I think we'll be lucky to find France again," he answered with the trace of a smile.

It was Massieu who spotted the deaf people. A man and a woman standing before a bake shop, their backs to the street. I didn't notice them. Their signs were small and hidden from our view.

I only saw a look of elation and relief pass over Massieu's face. He didn't even signal Abbé Sicard as he turned to speak with them. It was I who ran up to the abbé, poked his shoulder to break his stride, and pointed to Massieu, who had pulled another announcement from his pocket. He was deep in conversation with the deaf English people.

At first, they looked at him suspiciously. But, as soon as they realized that Massieu was as deaf as they, their faces changed. There was a lot of smiling, nodding, and gesturing.

Afraid that Massieu would have us engaged in a lengthy conversation, I went up to the group to explain our problem.

"Come this way," they gestured. "We'll show you."

Abbé Sicard was delighted with their offer. Together, the five of us walked quickly to the theater, which, it turned out, was not far away. Massieu and I took care to keep Abbé Sicard abreast of our conversation for he was as unable to understand the gestures of the deaf English as he was the words of the hearing ones.

They had four children, they explained, two of whom were deaf. The two deaf children were not in school. Tuition was expensive, but no, that was not why the children were not in school. The man made a good living taking care of property that his father owned. It was not the cost that made school out of reach for their children. Here, they paused and looked at each other.

"We're deaf," the woman finally stated. "The school doesn't accept children of deaf parents."

"Why?" I demanded, feeling my now well-trained sense of injustice mount.

"Signs," explained the man. "Signs are absolutely forbidden at that school and they know our children use them."

Massieu translated this for the abbé, who nodded. "A tragedy," he asserted, using his flamboyant theater signs. Massieu didn't have to translate that.

We watched as Abbé Sicard made a speech in signed French about how they should send their children to his school. Massieu translated it to gesture for the English couple, who simply couldn't believe that Paris had a school for the deaf where signs were used to teach.

"True, true," Massieu assured them.

I nodded my head for emphasis. For some reason I didn't want to tarnish the image that Abbé Sicard had presented by pointing out that the school was barely solvent and more children applied in a single month than could be admitted in a year.

"The French deaf are very lucky," they told us as we reached the theater. Massieu translated and Abbé Sicard nodded emphatically. We embraced in farewell. Despite our unplanned tour of the city, we were on time.

In a way, I liked arriving just before the performance began. It saved a lot of extra worry and tension. Massieu and I waited offstage for our part in the show.

"It's amazing how hard it is for the hearing to talk with each other when they don't know each other's speech," I commented to Massieu. He nodded, as he fastened the cloak that he insisted on wearing on stage.

Abbé Sicard opened the performance with an hour-long discourse about the virtues of sign language and how he had brought it to the deaf. Our English interpreter, the son of deaf parents, translated it for us with barely concealed amusement. The language of signs was international, Abbé Sicard said, shared by deaf people around the world. He gave, as an example, the deaf people who had helped us find the theater!

"They didn't use sign language," I remarked to Massieu.

"We used gestures," he agreed.

We would never have corrected Abbé Sicard, of course. We stood politely, watching him as he held forth, and waited for our cue.

"Really simple gestures," I elaborated. The English had coddled an imaginary infant, to show that they had a baby. They had held up three fingers and held their hands at successively higher heights to show us the ages of the other children. Their sign for *deaf* was easy to guess, flat open palm of the hand to the ear, then to the mouth. Our sign, forefinger to the ear and mouth was more graceful; their sign was more telling.

"Abbé Sicard seemed amazed that we understood them," I observed.

"Deaf communication always amazes the hearing," Massieu replied. "They think you need specific words to communicate."

I nodded.

"In some ways, the hearing admire us," Massieu continued. "In other ways, they patronize us. We deaf can communicate in mysterious international gestures, and yet we haven't enough brains to manage our own affairs."

During the performances, Massieu was eloquent; I was precise.

"What is eternity?" someone asked Massieu.

"A day without yesterday or tomorrow, a line that has no end," he answered.

"What is a difficulty?" another person asked.

"A possibility with an obstacle," Massieu responded.

Abbé Sicard told us later that the audience gasped at his answer. Then someone asked Massieu about God.

"Does God reason?" the Englishman wanted to know.

My former teacher did not even hesitate. "Man reasons because he doubts; he deliberates, he decides. God is omniscient. He never doubts; therefore, he never reasons."

Perhaps because of my youth, they asked me about women.

"Would you object to marrying an English lady?" someone wanted to know.

"As much an English lady as a French lady," I answered. That amused them greatly.

"Why?" my questioner persisted.

"Because I am not rich enough to support a wife and children," I answered. I saw them laugh and was glad I could be so entertaining, as well as truthful.

"Are deaf people unhappy?" still another person asked me.

"He who has never lost anything has no loss to regret," I responded. "Consequently, the deaf who have never spoken have never lost either hearing or speech, and, therefore, cannot lament either one or the other. Besides, it is a great consolation for them to be able to replace hearing by writing and speech by signs."

The next day, our interpreter read us the newspaper. It appeared that the English were very impressed by us—and by our sign language.

I couldn't imagine learning without sign language. How devastating teaching deaf students through mouth movements was, I learned from our visit to the English school.

Joseph Watson, nephew of the school's founder and its current director, was even more arrogant that Abbé Sicard. He didn't shake Massieu's hand, nor mine, but nodded to us, as if we were overgrown children. He was not very pleasant with the abbé either.

We toured the school; classes of deaf children stared curiously at us. We tried to wave to them, but even that brought frowns from our hosts.

"Is a wave considered a sign? Is that why it's forbidden?" Massieu asked our interpreter to ask Watson.

I don't know if Massieu's question was relayed or not. No answer was given.

I couldn't hear the students talk, of course. I just watched as their mouths contorted into shapes I had not seen since Abbé Magaron's speech class. I asked Abbé Sicard how they sounded.

"As though they were in pain," he answered.

I was surprised; it was unusual for him to be so blunt. Massieu asked our interpreter if he could understand them. In response, he bent forward and seemed to be listening intently.

"Mostly," he replied, after a few moments.

I tried to talk briefly with a small group of students. But they were nervous about using gestures in front of their teachers, so conversation was impossible.

One of them was bold enough to say something about us to his teacher. The teacher said some words to our interpreter and our interpreter translated them for us.

"They've never seen a deaf adult before," he told us.

All in all, it was a depressing day.

Napoléon had been defeated! Louis XVIII was back on his throne and it was safe for us to return to France. Massieu pointed to the words in the English newspaper and gave me the news.

"Are we going home?" I asked, not sure I was ready to give up our English adventure.

"No," he signed, regretfully. "We're staying another two weeks. There are still many people who want to see our performance."

I knew he missed our school and I felt badly for him. "It will be over soon." I told him, trying to comfort him.

What if we had left England when we planned to? What if Napoléon had been quickly defeated and we hadn't gone at all? My life would have been so different. For it was in England—during one of the last performances—that I met the man who would change my life.

He was the first American I had ever seen; I was not impressed. He was a little fellow with pursed lips and wire-rim glasses. I shook his hand politely, and he said, through our interpreter, that he had enjoyed our performance very much.

He was in England to learn how to teach the deaf, the interpreter told us.

"Before I saw your performance, I thought the deaf should learn to talk," the man said through our interpreter. "But after your performance tonight, I am convinced that signs must be used to teach the deaf children of America."

"Signs are the natural language of the deaf," Massieu told him.

Abbé Sicard walked up to join our conversation. With the abbé's arrival, the conversation swung quickly into voice and Massieu and I stood politely, waiting to be dismissed. Finally, the man shook each of our hands and turned to go.

"The English wanted him to pay a lot of money and work in their school for years before they let him learn how to teach the deaf," the abbé mumbled with his hands to Massieu, who always managed to understand him, and later explained all he said to me. "They also wanted him to promise to hire a member of their family when he started a school in America!"

"What arrogance!" Massieu exclaimed.

"I asked him to come to our school and learn in our country for free," Abbé Sicard told us.

He turned away, mumbling aloud now.

I remember asking the interpreter what the American's name was, for I had quickly forgotten it. "G-A-L-L-A-U-D-E-T," the interpreter spelled.

"Must be a French family that moved to America," suggested Massieu, noting the French spelling of the name.

But later, Massieu claimed that he didn't remember saying that. In fact, he told me he had forgotten the man and the name. I cannot remember much about the episode either.

17

The Preacher from America

Thomas Hopkins Gallaudet came to our school in mid-February in the midst of a winter rain. His clothes, not of the best quality, were wrinkled and wet. His hair was wet, too. He looked tired and a little sick.

He hadn't even changed his clothes after his long trip. He had arrived in Paris, dropped off his valise in a small room he had rented nearby, and commanded a cab to bring him immediately to the school.

He appeared briefly in my class with Abbé Sicard at his side. I knew that I'd seen him before, but I remembered our encounter in London only vaguely.

After class, Abbé Sicard introduced us again. Gallaudet's bearing was apologetic, not that of a man who thought himself of any worth. But his eyes said differently; behind tiny wire-rim glasses, they were lit with intelligence, curiosity, and even passion. He shook my hand firmly and stared directly into my eyes.

He must have done the same thing to Massieu.

"Gallaudet looked at me like he was taking my measure for some kind of suit," Massieu told me with a laugh.

His glasses became the basis for his name in signs. A "G" handshape held at the top of imaginary lenses, drawn back, and closed. It was a lot easier than spelling Gallaudet.

I became involved with him because he wanted to learn our signs. Abbé Sicard sent him to Massieu. Massieu decided that he would divide the task of teaching him with me.

We began the lessons immediately. We taught him classroom—or methodical—signs, of course. Like most hearing people, Gallaudet preferred that signs match as closely as possible the spoken word.

Massieu taught him verb tenses and worried about redoing the whole system for English verbs. I went through the alphabet with him and was pleased with how fast he learned it.

He began his classroom observations immediately, too. He started with the youngest students. When he was moved up to observe Massieu's class, my former teacher assured me that I would not be disappointed when he arrived in mine.

"He's a good signer, that American," he remarked.

"Excellent," I agreed, for I, too, had been impressed with his quick learning.

"He has a gift for pantomime," observed Massieu.

His face was expressive. For him, communication would not be limited to the hands. He would carry it with his body—to my delight as his teacher.

"It will serve him well when he returns to America," predicted Massieu.

If, academically, Gallaudet was brilliant, culturally, he was retarded. The man disliked Paris. He disliked the food; he disliked the wine ("With every meal? Surely, that is bad for your health."); he disliked the theaters. He even disapproved of the women.

Except for expeditions through the city, arranged formally by Abbé Sicard or on the spur of the moment by

Massieu and myself, and his visits to our school, the man never left his room.

"Paris is the capital of the world," I teased him.

"Paris is corrupt," he sighed.

"We have many beautiful cathedrals," added Massieu.

"And few people ever go inside," he countered.

"What about our wine?" I asked.

"To drink wine is wicked." He shook his head sadly as he looked at me.

"Wicked!" I would always shudder when he used that English word. He used it often. His biggest objection to Paris was not its noise, its dirt, or its business. My city was wicked because of its women.

"They are all going to destruction," he told me more than once.

"Whatever for?" I was totally perplexed.

"Lipcoloring," he signed. Then I was really confused.

"Lipcoloring?" I inquired.

"And rouge." He was serious.

"Rouge?"

Even more damning, "And they all drink wine."

Massieu finally explained to me; Gallaudet was a Puritan, he said.

"A Puritan?"

"It's a religion," Massieu began.

At first, I thought he was mistaken.

"He is a Congregationalist," I corrected, my fingers slipping over the letters of the unfamiliar word. Trying to sort out the labels of Protestant religious groups was an art in itself.

"Yes," Massieu allowed, "he is, strictly speaking, a Congregationalist. But Congregationalists are descendants of those first Americans, the Puritans, who fled to America more than two hundred years ago to live out their strict interpretation of what they thought it meant to be Christian."

I had heard of Puritans.

"Their name comes from the word 'pure'," I ventured. "He calls Abbé Sicard a heathen," I added.

"And Abbé Sicard calls him a heathen," Massieu laughed.

He was right to find all this funny. Like me, he avoided religious topics with both men. For both of us, it seemed silly for grown men to fuss about these tiny points of dogma. There was one God and one Savior. I was always unclear exactly what the division was about. Massieu and I humored them both.

I grinned.

"Good thing no one asked you to define 'Puritan' in London," I told him.

Gallaudet said little about his own life, but asked me questions constantly about mine. How had I become deaf? At what age? Did I find the abbé's method successful in the classroom? When had I started to study English? Did I have brothers and sisters? Did I read the Bible?

When I asked him questions, he answered directly but without details. It was almost as if he were embarrassed when he talked about himself.

He told me that he had gone to a school called "Yale." But it was Massieu who told me that Yale was not just a school, but a university, and that it was very well-respected. Further, Massieu said that Gallaudet had been the youngest student in his class, and that he had gotten the highest grades.

"He may look stupid, he may act stupid," smiled my former teacher, "but stupid, no. He's not stupid."

I asked Gallaudet how he liked being a minister. He said that he liked it, although he had health problems that had forced him into business for a short while. Finally, I asked him how he had become interested in deafness.

"I was enchanted by a deaf girl," he smiled. I guess my return smile was a little too quick.

"No, no," he said, understanding my meaning quickly and just as quickly correcting me.

"The girl is only a child, nine years old. She's the daughter of a neighbor."

Here he dropped the pen that we used to converse half in English, half in French, to practice his finger-spelling. "A-L-I-C—"

I used my own hand to re-form his "C" and he began again.

"A-L-I-C-E." He made each letter carefully.

"Alice," I read the name easily. "Be careful to hold your wrist still as your fingers form the letters."

He nodded. Then he took a deep breath and spelled slowly and clearly, her family name. "C-O-G-S-W-E-L-L."

She was lovely, he made me understand, using neither fingerspelling, nor pen, but communicating clearly in gestures. She was smart and curious, and it broke his heart that, after falling sick at two years of age, she had been cut off from other people because the illness had left her deaf.

"She must learn about God," he exclaimed with sudden passion.

Like Abbé Sicard and the founders of our school, his purpose in teaching the deaf was to tell us about God, put us in touch with our Christian heritage, enable us to take the sacraments, and save our souls.

At first, Gallaudet said he had wanted Alice—and

the other deaf children of America—to speak, and through speaking, to teach them.

"I thought that it would be easier to tell them about God if they could read it on my lips," he told me. "I thought that speaking would make them whole."

That's why he had gone to England first, where the schools were strictly oral and forbade signs and sign language.

The English had received him coldly, almost hostilely, as they had received the abbé, Massieu, and myself.

"I was very disappointed," he shook his head.

"Massieu said that the English attached absurd conditions to teaching you their method," I commented.

He nodded wearily.

As it seemed to me that I worked under conditions that were also more than a bit absurd, I asked him if he could tell me what the conditions were.

He began listing them: "That I teach and work at the school six and a half days a week—from seven in the morning to eight in the evening; that I wait for each student to completely learn the skill I taught before I could learn how to teach the next skill—"

"But that is truly unacceptable!" Without meaning to, I had cut him off. "That means, in effect, that you would have to wait for the entire education of one student. Five years?" I asked.

"Three years," he answered. "I had to agree to stay three years."

Gallaudet shook his head. "The deaf children of America can't wait that long."

But that was not all. He also had to promise to take someone from England back with him to work in the American school. And perhaps hire a relative of the director who was already in America.

"It was outrageous!" he exclaimed.

As we communicated more and more, it became apparent to me that he was not the gentle self-effacing person he appeared at first glance.

Gallaudet had spent several months trying to understand what the English teachers did without committing himself to a three-year stay. Finally, he had given up. He was putting his hopes in the French method.

"Now I thank God for the contrariness, the narrow-mindedness, and the outright greed of the English," he stated, with a rare smile. "It brought me to you."

"You are convinced about the worth of signs?" I asked him.

He nodded. "For two reasons," he added eagerly.

Gallaudet had gone to Scotland to visit an oral school. As so often happens, in search of one lesson, he learned another. What impressed Gallaudet in Scotland was not the oral school, but a Scottish professor who hated oralism.

"His name is Dugald Stewart. He's a professor of philosophy at the University of Edinburgh. He abhors oralism." Gallaudet smiled at me, for already he knew that I, too, disliked oralism. "He says the art of teaching speech should be reserved for training parrots."

"You don't need to be a philosophy professor to think that," I answered.

Gallaudet nodded.

"We also talked a lot about language—what it is in us humans that makes it possible." He paused a moment.

"Speech is not language, Clerc," he observed gravely. "If Stewart is right, the oralists are committing a crime against humanity and a crime against God."

It was my turn to smile. None of this was a revelation for me. "And the second reason?" I asked him.

"Why, seeing you and Massieu, of course," he answered. "The proof—if such proof were needed."

Gallaudet was sick again. And, again, he was trying to hide it. He couldn't. He was pale and coughing when he entered my classroom, and his eyes watery and pink with a low-grade fever.

When I asked him how he was taking care of himself, it came out that he was really doing nothing to help his body heal.

He had started feeling bad the day before, he told me. As it was Sunday, he had gone to bed "as soon as he could."

"Which meant you dragged yourself to church," I chided.

"I had to preach," he explained sheepishly.

"Preach? Why did you have to preach? Surely there are other English-speaking preachers," I scolded him gently. "The American churchgoers in Paris survived before you came here and they'll survive after you're gone."

He smiled weakly and pulled out some words he had listed. He wanted to know the signs for *work, savior, carriage, wheel,* and *justice.*

"We're still working on the most basic signs," I interrupted him. "We'll get to those." I had to stop mid-sentence for he had a fit of coughing.

"Wasn't the voyage here difficult for you?" I couldn't help asking him. His health was so fragile.

It was indeed difficult, he told me, smothering another fit of coughing. He was putting his trust in God that it would not be fatal.

"That's why I need to finish here quickly," he added. "In fact, I'm getting ready to go home."

"You've only been here five weeks!" I protested. "It's not enough time."

An American friend recently had arrived in Paris, Gallaudet told me, and they had spent the weekend reminiscing. Now his old homesickness was back, sharp and aching in his Protestant American soul.

"I must get started Clerc." His gestures were urgent.

"You want to stop learning and start teaching," I responded gently.

18

Leaving St. Jacques?

Gallaudet worked frantically to complete his tasks. He stayed all day in my classroom, talked with Massieu and myself right through the dinner hour, and took material home to read.

"But I'm still not ready!" he cried one afternoon. "I understand you and I understand Massieu. But I still don't always understand the students. How will I teach deaf students if I can't understand them?"

I understood his frustration and disappointment.

"You will understand them," I told him. "You learn very quickly."

"Perhaps," he replied. "But right now I help no one. I am less useful here than—" He stopped, unable to come up with a word.

"An orchestra," I joked, trying to cheer him. He would not be cheered.

"If only you could write me a book of all you know," he sighed. "A book of signs, a book of teaching verbs, a book of adverbs . . ."

My mood had changed as he talked. I was ready to broach my idea.

"Perhaps I could go with you."

He was stunned.

I looked at him squarely to let him know I was serious.

"You've learned a lot," I continued, "but two months is not enough time. Neither is four months. You didn't learn English in four months and you won't learn signs in four months, either.

"If we went back to America together, you would have at least one trained teacher for your deaf students. I could also continue to teach you."

I paused a moment, looking at his face. His eyes had widened at the audacity of my suggestion.

"I could be your assistant."

I knew that he had rejected the idea of taking an English assistant; now I was suggesting a deaf French one.

"You could leave almost immediately," I added persuasively.

"Could you leave here?" he asked. "Could you really leave?"

My gaze did not waver.

"Yes," I answered simply. "It would be difficult. Leaving would be difficult. But, yes, I could leave here."

"I'll think about it," he answered in gestures slower than usual.

My heart tightened a notch. I had had experience with the thinking of the clergy. I resolved not to let myself hope. Of course, I hoped anyway.

"Clerc, come look!"

Two days later, I arrived in my classroom to find Gallaudet already there. Never had I seen him so overjoyed.

"What is it?" I asked, almost worried at his levity.

He had received a letter from his American student, Alice Cogswell. He held it out to me and I admired the childish writing. I understood some of the English words, too: "beautiful," "mama," "boy."

Gallaudet had already translated it into French for me. He provided her father's introduction in signs, then handed me the translation of Alice's own work.

"My Dear Sir—I remember story Mrs. Sigourney was tell me. Old many years, Mr. Colt little boy Name man Peter Colt very much curls little boy hair Oh! beautiful mama lap little boy comb curl love—"

Gallaudet apologized for the grammar. It was not necessary, I motioned, and continued reading.

"—little boy head very cold mama tie handkerchief warm, tears no more mama very sorry—"

It was a story that her teacher had read in class. I was impressed by a father who knew better than to correct his child's first attempts to write.

"I love you very much," it ended.

"It's a beautiful letter," I told Gallaudet.

In a small, private school in America, Alice was proving to be a bright child who learned quickly. She was impatiently awaiting Gallaudet's return.

My students began to arrive. Over the translation of the letter, I watched them enter and stand by their desks. They wouldn't sit down until I bid them "good day" and gave them permission.

Still at my arm, Gallaudet tugged at my sleeve. It was unusual for him to distract me from my class. I supposed he was so excited about the child's letter that he could not help himself.

I tried to hide my annoyance as I turned to look at him.

"Clerc," he demanded urgently, apologetically. He knew that I resented his interfering with my work in the classroom.

"My friend is leaving soon," he signed.

I stiffened and turned away. I felt vaguely embarrassed about the proposal that I had made to go with him. Neither of us had talked about it since. Now he would depart, too soon, and alone. But his departure, like his arrival, was not my business.

"Bonjour class," I signed to my waiting students.

I watched Gallaudet. Actually, I couldn't ignore him. He was waving Alice's letter slightly to get my attention. Thoroughly irritated, I turned again to him, standing next to the first row of students. Knowing I was annoyed, he glanced downward, embarrassed.

"You would never treat Abbé Sicard that way," Massieu gently scolded me in my imagination. It's funny how Abbé Sicard treated me as though he were better than I—and I resented the treatment even while I accepted it. Gallaudet treated me as an equal and as his teacher—and I accepted that, too.

He had flipped Alice's letter over and was writing a message on it. Curiosity got the better of me. I waited for him to finish.

He did. Looking up, excited and smiling, he caught my eyes immediately. Seeing the students' eyes on him, too, he had no choice but to hold up his message. It stood out in large letters, one sentence in French, one sentence in English.

"I want you to come with me to America."

I was not quite able to believe my eyes.

"Talk later," he signed.

I nodded.

"Bonjour, class," I signed again to my eight top-level students.

"Bonjour, Mr. Clerc," they signed back in polite unison.

"Please be seated," I finally directed.

With that my knees gave out, and I sat down, too.

After class, Gallaudet told me excitedly that he had thought a long time about my proposal to accompany him. It was a good idea. He was sure of it. He had prayed and God had affirmed his decision.

"You will be my teacher and a teacher for American students. You will show everyone instantly how successful signing is for teaching deaf students." He was talking and signing in such excitement that I almost couldn't understand him.

We would draw up a contract. He wanted me to promise to stay in America for at least three years.

"Clerc, Hartford is a beautiful place. But, if you are not happy in my country, you will not have to stay," he promised me earnestly.

He built paragraphs of signs and gestures in the air and paragraphs of words on paper, as if he had to persuade me even as he laid out the plan.

I had no second thoughts. In earnest, I had made the proposal; in earnest, I accepted it. Nevertheless, alarm coursed through my body. I could hardly believe, or trust, my good fortune.

"You didn't want to take an Englishman," I reminded him. "Why are you interested in me?"

"Those English couldn't really help me," he said. "You can. When people meet you, they will surely give money to the school. You are proof of the sanctity of my cause."

"I'll have to get Abbé Sicard's permission," I said, as if in a trance. "And I need time to say good-bye to my mother."

He agreed immediately.

I wrote a letter immediately to Abbé Sicard. Excitedly, I told Massieu and Bébian. Pierrot and Claude had come by and we were eating together at a café near the school.

"A barbarian country," exclaimed Bébian.

"Indians," added Claude, shaking his head.

"Puritans," remembered Bébian.

"Russia is poor," Massieu commented, "but at least the Russian Orthodox faith is civilized."

I was exasperated with them. They had missed the point.

"Can't you see the importance of this?" I demanded.

They responded with countless petty objections to my going, countless meaningless reasons to stay at St. Jacques. There was no talking to them.

"Why are you so quiet?" I demanded suddenly of Pierrot. He had sat down as excited as a boy waiting for a rich uncle to bring him presents from a foreign trip, but had fallen still on learning my news.

He shook his head as if befuddled.

"I guess I'll just miss you," he admitted finally. "And I'm sorry you'll miss my wedding."

"Wedding!" The three of us turned to him.

"Who?"

"When?"

"Is she deaf?"

Pierrot only laughed at us.

"Deaf and beautiful," he responded, grinning.

But he was mysterious about who she was. We would know her, he told us. We would see her when he brought her by the school, which he planned to do next week.

"Is it possible you'll still be here for the wedding?" he looked at me inquisitively. The wedding was months away.

"I doubt it," I told him. "I've already written to Abbé Sicard. After he gives me permission to go, I need to see my mother. I've already started to pack."

I had just finished the letter to my mother telling her of my impending visit when Abbé Sicard responded to my request. I stared at his letter in disbelief.

He accused me of being stubborn, spiteful, and ungrateful. Each characteristic, he railed, would justify not only letting me go, but avidly kicking me out. But my faults were not as pronounced as his, Abbé Sicard's, goodness. I wanted to go to a Protestant land and live in a town where there was no Catholic church? Having labored so hard to save my soul, he would not have me trifle with it now. In his best conscience, the abbé could not let me leave the school.

A slight movement caught my eye and I looked up to see Gallaudet's silhouette at my door. He must have known what the letter said.

"I'm sorry, Clerc." He looked genuinely distressed.

I watched his face, trying to hide my pain.

"Are you going to accept this?" I demanded.

His eyes turned to the floor for a moment, then returned to my face. He said nothing.

"Did you talk with him?" I asked at last.

"He told me you were too valuable to leave the school," replied Gallaudet gently. "I am really sorry."

"He said nothing like that here," I gestured to the paper still in my hands. But I couldn't bring myself to tell Gallaudet what the letter said.

"He has Massieu—" I began, but caught myself in midsentence. It was no use arguing with this good but accepting man whose future had always been assured. I excused myself and left the room.

I walked off the school grounds without asking for permission or even telling anyone that I was leaving. I followed the long twisting street down to the river Seine, and followed the Seine until the shops of Paris gave way to houses, and the houses gave way to small fields.

My thoughts would not stop. Nor would my anger.

He's got Massieu, I thought watching the ducks swimming parallel to me. And Gallaudet is always sick!

I was exasperated. There are even more reasons for me to go to America than there were for me to go to Russia, I continued my angry diatribe.

I was careful not to sign to myself as I had seen other deaf people do when thoughts raced through their heads. I walked with my head bent forward and my fingers clenched tightly in my palms.

I recognized Abbé Sicard's words for what they were. Hearing hubris, nothing more. I was not hurt. I was infuriated.

Finally, I stopped walking and faced the Seine. I vowed to oppose him.

My head straightened and my fingers relaxed. The ducks stroked smoothly onward in the direction of the setting sun.

I wrote back to Abbé Sicard as soon as I returned to the school, slashing the words across the page. I pointed out all I had done and tried to do for him. I reminded him of the trip to Russia.

"You helped Jauffret," I wrote, reminding him of the teacher whose voyage he had sanctioned. "Now help me."

I reminded him that Jean Massieu would remain on his staff and implied that maybe Gallaudet would deprive the school of Massieu if he were not allowed to take me.

"Losing me is nothing compared with what losing Massieu would be," I noted.

I carefully and neatly copied the letter over. Then I carried it to Abbé Sicard personally.

Usually the secretary took all his correspondence and screened his unexpected visitors. I swept past him, rapped purposefully on the abbé's door, opened it, and entered.

He blushed when he saw me, then paled when he read the letter. I don't know what he said. I was too upset to decipher his lips and signs. I just watched— and waited for him to stop. When he finally did, I didn't answer him, having not understood him, nor did I try to justify myself.

"Let me go," I insisted, not angrily, but with a firmness I hadn't known I possessed.

He flushed and recommenced his monologue. I watched him. When he paused again, I repeated my statement.

"Let me go," I signed.

So red that I was afraid he would faint, he began again a tirade in signs. Again, I waited. And, again, I met his first pause with the same three signs.

"Let me go."

Finally, he threw up his hands.

"I will be dead when you return," he cried.

It was his surrender. He was beaten. I scarcely stayed to reassure him. I wanted to find Gallaudet. I wanted to finish packing. I was free.

19

"Of Course Clerc Must Go"

I make it sound easy. It was, none of it, easy.

Though I rarely saw my mother and we communicated mostly through letters, it hurt me to tell her about my plans. My father had died the year before and she was still in mourning. I felt I was adding to her sadness.

I meant it when I told her that, if I could have postponed my trip for a year, I would. But I had no choice. Gallaudet had already made the reservations. The ship would leave in a few days.

I promised her I would write. I promised her I would remain a Catholic and keep the sacraments. I told her that I would only stay for three years. But my words felt empty and useless even as I wrote them.

She had known already of my decision, she told me. The abbé had written her. And he had begged her to talk me out of it. My mother, as devoutly Catholic as any priest, was no more happy than Abbé Sicard to see her son go to a land of Protestants.

She understood none of my words about destiny and duty. She could have cared less about the deaf in America. She cared about only one deaf person, she told me tearfully, and he was here before her.

François and his wife and children came to see me off. Actually, many of the people of La Balme came.

They stood smiling in our yard, near the waiting carriage. I had gone from outcast to hero overnight. I cannot say I minded the change.

François supported my trip to America. "Of course Clerc must go," he had told my mother only the night before. "You should be proud of him."

"I'll take care of her," he told me now, his arm linked through my mother's.

As I left my village, thinking it was perhaps for the last time, I remembered my leave-taking as a boy, going I knew not where—or why. Now I knew where I was going—and why.

The hardest good-bye was still to come.

"Thank you very much," I told my students when they presented me with a farewell card. My signs were formal and self-conscious. After longing to go for so long, suddenly I found it hard to think about leaving St. Jacques.

The party was supposed to be a small one, but it seemed that half of the school had crowded into my small classroom. Abbé Sicard, his once-full chin now an empty bag of wrinkles, stood next to Massieu, who arrived bedecked in new clothing and brandishing many watches. Bébian, his face smiling and flushed, was there, too. They were all watching Gallaudet, who was holding forth about his plans for the returning to America, his latest letter from Alice held proudly in his hand.

"Pierrot's bringing his fiance!" Massieu used quick and tiny signs as Pierrot and his wife-to-be entered the room arm in arm, their faces alight, even triumphant.

"Marie Catherine!" My mouth dropped, my heart turned over, and my hands froze. The woman I had once loved and believed cloistered forever in a home for the poor, was going to become my friend's wife.

Claude and I took turns kissing her cheeks.

"You look lovely," I told her. "Lovely."

"How? How?" Claude ever gentle, couldn't frame a polite way to ask Pierrot how he had managed to secure himself this woman.

"My uncle," Pierrot answered swiftly, permitting Abbé Sicard to escort Marie Catherine to the doorway to greet the still-arriving guests. "He offered her employment in his home."

"And he let her marry you?" Claude slapped Pierrot on the back.

"Well, he went to her family and explained the situation. Her family is nice, but poor. Very poor. I think they preferred her to be with me than at the home." He paused a minute, then added with his characteristic honesty, "And, of course, they liked the money."

"Your uncle paid them?" I was horrified.

"As good an investment as school for sure!" smiled Massieu.

I wanted to inch my way over and talk with Marie Catherine, but I was surrounded by students and former students, and it was impossible to move. Ferdinand Berthier was there. Claudius Forestier had walked from across town. Even Allibert had come to the party. As I looked around, the only student missing was Alexander Machowitz, the passionate young count, whom I loved like a son.

Alex was the only person who had not even tried to appear to be happy when I announced my decision to the class. He didn't care that American deaf needed someone like me, he said. He didn't care that Massieu would remain. He cared only that his favorite teacher was leaving him. His face froze in a frown. He wanted me to stay.

Yesterday, he had sought me out after class to argue with me about my upcoming journey. I tried again to explain to him the importance of my trip, why I had to go. He would have none of it.

"You don't like us!" he accused. "You never liked your deaf students!"

"Alex, please . . ." I could see it was no use.

He tried to hit me.

"Alex!" My hand grabbed his.

"I hate you!" he cried.

Using all my strength, I tried to hold him with one hand and sign with the other. I couldn't. He broke free again and again. Finally, I turned my back to walk away. With the strength of youth and fury, he grabbed my shoulders and turned me back to face him.

"You are a fake deaf!" He was crying now. "Everyone says so. You are a fake deaf—"

I was surprised how his words stung me. I grabbed him and shook him, harder than I meant to. When I released him, he fell to the floor. I looked at him a moment, sobbing, his arms finally at rest, and then I left. I was too shaken to stay.

I couldn't bear his hurt. It felt too much like my own.

"Where's Alex?" I asked Berthier now.

"In bed," he answered.

"He won't get up," added Forestier.

"He signed the card," Claude assured me, worried at my expression.

He pointed to the signature. Above it, Alex had scrawled a single sentence, the only message on the card.

"Alex loves Clerc," it said.

I pulled my eyes away quickly. I couldn't let myself think about this.

"You have a loyal correspondent," I signed through my students to Gallaudet, gesturing toward the letter from Alice he held in his hand.

He nodded, as I knew he would, and ambled over to read it to me.

"You must realize she has no help with these letters," Gallaudet was telling anyone who would pay attention. "They are entirely her own."

"She's very bright for a nine-year-old," commented Massieu approvingly.

"Especially considering her schooling," harrumphed Abbé Sicard.

Gallaudet read us the letter, translating the words into signs so quickly that even I, his teacher, was astonished. She must have written other things, too, but what my eyes saw and my brain remembers was this:

"I am not good heart," the young American wrote. "I wish good heart, so very want, I am feeling bad, very sorry. God made me deaf and dumb. Perhaps me very bad, I hear not. God Jesus Christ know best and God make all."

It was too much. The Puritans had their ropes of guilt around the child's soul. A wave of sadness washed through me and tears sprang to my eyes.

Gallaudet misunderstood the cause of my emotion.

"Clerc, you will help her know God's love," he told me.

I shook my head, wanting to leave, but unsure how. I was grateful that the students were talking among themselves and paying no attention to us.

Massieu, as always, shared my mood. Suddenly, he hugged me and pressed a watch into my hand.

"It's new," he told me. "Gold. From Switzerland. You keep it."

Too overwhelmed to thank him, I could only clutch the watch, and look at him helplessly. What craziness possessed me to want to leave this place? The loss was too great.

"Other schools are necessary," continued my first teacher, almost in tears himself. "Without other schools, there would be no Abbé Sicard." He tried to smile.

"And no Jean Massieu."

But the sadness was too much. I turned away to hide my tears.

Again, Gallaudet misunderstood.

"You'll learn English, Clerc," he said excitedly, touching my sleeve to get my attention. He looked around to the others.

"Already he astounds me with what he knows," he commented.

But of course it wasn't improving my English or the Indians or the Puritans. It was none of that. It was Alice Cogswell, writing about a deity that would make her deaf. And Alex Machowitz, crying in an empty dormitory. And a new watch in my sweaty hand. It was the enormity. Leaving St. Jacques, my love for it intensified.

Feeling I could stand no more of this, I headed for the door.

"It's only a matter of time," Gallaudet was saying.

Across the room, I could see Berthier with the other students. His signs jumped out at me.

"I'll tell you why he's going," my brightest student was saying, as if he were accepting a dare. "I'll tell you why if you want to know."

He paused as more of us turned to look at him.

"Because there's still nothing for the deaf in America. No schools. No teachers. Nothing. Gallaudet can't do it alone. He has a good heart, perhaps, but that isn't enough. No one ever gave a man money to start a school just because he had a good heart. They'll believe in the school when they meet Laurent Clerc."

Everyone's eyes turned to me as Berthier pointed to me standing near the doorway. "When they meet Clerc, that's when they'll give money."

As usual, the other students fell still while Berthier talked. I myself stopped my flight to watch him, entranced and distracted entirely from the other conversations that flowed around me and my own profound sorrow.

"And after the American deaf get a school, then what?" Berthier demanded of the other students. "Gallaudet can't teach. Gallaudet can't sign. It's Clerc who will teach. It's Clerc who will teach the students—and the teachers."

Berthier shook his head in frustration with his cohorts, or perhaps with all of us.

"Two generations of a bit of schooling for a few deaf in this country, and we start to think everyone knows that education is our natural right. And that we will be given it *because* it is our right."

From the corner of my eye, I caught sight of Massieu, who was also watching Berthier. We exchanged amazed glances. How that boy knew what he knew was a mystery. But Berthier was not finished.

"Clerc's a bridge between our school and a new school yet-to-be in America. Clerc is our gift to the deaf of America. You know what Abbé Sicard calls him? The Apostle to the Deaf in the New World!

"You watch. Clerc's school will educate hundreds, maybe thousands, of deaf Americans—and those deaf, yes, those American deaf, will make the French deaf stronger. It will happen."

Finally, he stopped. Massieu and I and every student in the room had watched him, amazed at his understanding and passion. Massieu and I exchanged glances again, wondering at this student who was growing up within our walls.

"What did he say?" Abbé Sicard asked, his head bobbing back and forth between Massieu and myself.

I was too busy with my own thoughts to answer him. Berthier was right, of course. François was right, too. I had to go. It was my destiny.

With the back of my hand, I wiped away tears that had splashed from my eyes and down my cheeks. I walked out of the room.

Afterword

Ferdinand Berthier was right. Laurent Clerc's decision to accompany Gallaudet to America and help him set up a school for deaf children had immeasurable consequences. The school founded by Gallaudet and Clerc fostered the growth of an educated, signing deaf community in the United States—a community that would one day lead the world in demanding recognition for deaf people as members of a rich minority community with beautiful sign languages all their own. Clerc's French signs mingled with those of his deaf students to produce much of the idiom in today's American Sign Language.

But as Clerc left his homeland, all of this was far in the future. Back in Paris, Abbé Sicard remained director of the St. Jacques school until his death, probably from old age, in 1822. Ferdinand Berthier, who wanted so much to emulate Clerc, became a noted scholar, reading widely in many languages and writing several books and many professional articles. Berthier became dean of the faculty at St. Jacques and established what was probably the first formal deaf club in the world.

Claudius Forestier, the student who almost died from his "treatment" for deafness, also went on to write several books, including books on deaf education and religious poetry for children. Forestier and his hearing wife became principal and matron of a newly established school for the deaf in Lyon, where, to Clerc's consternation, Forestier neither hired nor affiliated with any other hearing person, making his school possibly the first school in the world to have an entirely deaf staff.

Not much is known about Claude Wallon, Clerc's classmate with undisputed artistic talent. One of Wallon's paintings of the founder of St. Jacques, Abbé de l'Epee, was exhibited during the bicentennial celebration of the school. The school still stands where it did in Clerc's day, on the rue St. Jacques on the Left Bank of Paris.

Still less is known about Françoise Desprès and Marie Catherine Companie. Both girls were admitted to the girls' school when Clerc was a student. Françoise—deemed by Abbé Salvan, head of the girls' school, to be "well disposed" to learn—was dismissed from the school for "scandalous morals." Pierrot Janty, Clerc's outspoken monitor and the only fictional character in the book, was modeled on Pierre Desloges, a deaf man, never a student at St. Jacques, who published an eloquent defense of sign language in 1779.

Jean Massieu, the gifted teacher of Clerc, married after Abbé Sicard's death and became principal of a school for the deaf in Lille, a city in the north of France. Allibert, the hard-of-hearing boy who was separated from his schoolmates and whisked into the home of the school's doctor to communicate exclusively through speech and lipreading, rejected oralism as an adult. He wrote that "sign language is as essential for our minds as air is for our respiration."

Roch-Ambrose Bébian, one of the few hearing people who had the genius to recognize and respect the sign language of his deaf students and coworkers and the passion to advocate relentlessly and sometimes tactlessly for them, was dismissed from his job at St. Jacques. Bébian wrote a book on deaf education—asked to do so by the same administrators who had dismissed him—before he left for Guadaloupe, where he died at the age of forty-five.

Laurent Clerc would become financially comfortable in his adopted America, teaching at the school—today's American School for the Deaf, the oldest continually operating school for the deaf in this country—until his retirement. He married one of his students, Elizabeth Boardman, and they had six children. He died in 1869 at eighty-three years of age.